Bronze Age Textiles

DUCKWORTH DEBATES IN ARCHAEOLOGY

Series editor: Richard Hodges

Bronze Age Textiles

Klavs Randsborg

Bristol Classical Press

First published in 2011 by
Bristol Classical Press
an imprint of
Bloomsbury Academic
Bloomsbury Publishing Plc
36 Soho Square
London W1D 3QY

CIP records for this book are available from the
British Library and the Library of Congress

ISBN 978-0-7156-4078-4

Typeset by Ray Davies
Printed and bound in Great Britain by
CPI Antony Rowe, Chippenham and Eastbourne

www.bloomsburyacademic.com

Contents

Contents

Preface

Among its prized collections, the Danish National Museum holds completely preserved woollen dresses, both female and male, from the Early Bronze Age (the late second millennium BC). These garments are matched in old age and superb preservation only by finds from Ancient Egypt.

This study is based on the highly professional and very thorough textile investigations by Margrethe Hald (1897-1982) at the National Museum, Copenhagen (Broholm & Hald 1929-35; 1939; 1940; cf. Hald 1950; [1980]). Later studies of these Bronze Age textiles have provided more data and much inspiration to the author, as have other textile studies and related investigations. More than two generations after Margarethe Hald, it is time to reconsider these Bronze Age textiles and place them in their wider European setting.

Among recent studies are the important investigations by Professor Lise Bender Jørgensen, University of Trondhjem, Norway, discussing the very many fragments of textiles that have come down to us from the Bronze and Iron Ages. Most of these fragments have been preserved by metal oxides emanating from bronze and other metal grave gifts (Bender Jørgensen 1986; 1992). Only rarely do the fragments tell us much about the dresses, but they do inform us about cloth types and weaving. Also, the fragments are well dated and widely distributed in both time and space, while Early Bronze Age dresses are restricted to Jylland (Jutland).

This study may be considered a sequel to a recent publication of the Early Bronze Age oak-coffin graves which contained the complete dresses, among many other items (Randsborg &

7

Christensen 2006). That work was written with a view to social dimensions and cosmology, as well as the power of precise dendro-chronological dating.

In most graves from the Nordic Bronze Age we are left merely with the bronze (and gold) items, some pottery, other solid artefacts, and, perhaps, human bones. We tend to down-play, even forget, about the homespun textiles for the better preserved metals like gold and bronze, often in form of exotic artefacts arriving from far away in the case of Denmark. This understandable ignorance even has a gender dimension, with metalwork being a male occupation, and textiles a female one.

The well-preserved textiles of the oak-coffin graves open a door on the beauty and riches of textiles in the historical, social and cultural understanding of the Bronze Age, as well as individuals and their lives. As grave gifts, textiles would often have been more valuable than bronzes commonly buried with the dead. In the Ancient Civilisations of the Eastern Mediterranean, textiles were generally much more costly than foodstuffs, materials, animals, bronzes, and many other items; it is likely that the same was the case throughout prehistoric Europe.

Observations by the present author include renewed inspection of the Bronze Age and other textiles and related data, like images and figurines, throughout Europe, as well as archaeological, ethnographical, and historical information, often sampled beyond Europe.

Acknowledgements for information go to Professor Anthony Harding; Lone Hvass, MagArt; Flemming Kaul, DrPhil; Finn Ole Nielsen, DrHC; Drs Klaus Tidow; Volker Hilberg; Karina Grömer; and for assistance to Dr Inga Merkyte. I am obliged to Bristol Classical Press for accepting the work for its Debates in Archaeology series.

The volume is dedicated to Richard Hodges in appreciation of his archaeological and historical vision, sense of field projects, and administrative talent.

Klavs Randsborg

1

Issues

Danish Early Bronze Age woollen textiles were met with wonder when found in the nineteenth and twentieth centuries, but perhaps less so than one would have expected due to the equally rich material of garments from the Iron Age. Nearly all of the archaeologists were men, none of them with professional knowledge of the technical aspects of textiles. M. Hald's work in the 1930s added this dimension (Broholm & Hald 1929-35; 1939; 1940; cf. Hald 1950; [1980]), but, like the studies of her male colleagues, lacked social understanding of the graves or a broader perspective. One reason is that few finds are known from the bridging Late Bronze Age, but the main one is the rather provincial outlook of the archaeology of the period between the two World Wars and the post-World War II years. The result was that the Bronze Age garments were merely placed in the golden light of a golden age (research history in Jensen 1998).

The garments themselves posed various problems. The male ones were but few; men were dressed in coat or loincloth and cloak and wore thick war caps (a pixie cap was added among the grave gifts). Until the Egtved woman was found in the 1920s (Thomsen 1929-35), the women were believed to have worn blouses and long, very heavy skirts, or wraps. The young Egtved woman was dressed in blouse and a short string skirt that stunned the period. Some German archaeologists even identified her as a 'dancer' from the Balkans or equipped her with a long skirt she did not wear in the grave. Clearly a woman of the great Nordic race could not wear such a revealing skirt. It is an irony that a wrap was actually included in the

9

Egtved grave as a cover. Some archaeologists have argued that the string skirt is either a young girl's skirt or a summer garment; recently it has even been claimed that the string skirt was a cultic dress on the basis of figurines showing very short string skirts on otherwise naked acrobatic dancers.

The find of the young Skrydstrup woman in the 1930s added to the questions, since she was buried in a very large, very heavy wrap strapped with a rather thin belt (Broholm & Hald 1939). Reconstructions show her in this 'large skirt' that would have constantly fallen to the ground (underwear as such was not used, at least to judge from the textiles found in graves); a later idea was that the skirt would have been worn under the armpits, but if so, movement would have been severely hampered. The simple solution follows below: women did not wear the 'large skirts' as skirts but as wraps. If not donning string skirts, they would have worn the smaller long plain skirts that are also present in the graves but traditionally regarded as 'blankets'.

Today, archaeology enables estimates of the season of burial to be made, and thus aids in the discussion of summer versus winter garments. It also allows for a detailed understanding of the social roles and positions of the buried, as measured by the grave goods and – in unique cases – by the textiles. New garments have been identified, like female sanitary napkins and 'shopping bags'. The amounts of labour-consuming textiles in the graves must have been high, especially in the case of women, while the male graves contained more of the metals. At any rate, we assume a particular role for the women in producing the textiles.

Bender Jørgensen, by studying fragments of textiles preserved in quite large numbers of Bronze and Iron Age graves, has added to our recent knowledge (Bender Jørgensen 1986; 1992) as well as giving an overview of the research situation in Denmark, concerning the instruments used, for instance, as well as of parts of Central Europe and even beyond. Only a limited number of textile fragments are known from Europe beyond Denmark: a few, mainly linens, from the British Isles, a few more from Spain (linens), and scattered finds from Central Europe, both linens and woollen fabrics, including a number of new woollen finds from Austria (Grömer 2007). Woollen textiles do not seem to be that common and may represent luxury articles. European linen clothing is known from the Neolithic, for instance in Switzerland, as are garments in fur and hide.

Bronze Age Greece saw considerable production of woollen textiles, as demonstrated by the Linear B texts, we even get a grasp on the mechanisms of production and control, but virtually no textiles have been preserved from the region. The few that we have are of linen, as in other parts of the Mediterranean, for instance Spain. The Balkans, like the Aegean, supply a number of figurines with dress details, like a female blouse and a long, often voluminous, skirt. Images, including wall paintings from Greek palaces, are another rich source on dress.

Against this sparse background, the woollen textiles and garments of the North are truly outstanding and deserve much more attention than they have received hitherto. Bender Jørgensen, writing partly in English, does not discuss the full garments, and Hald's works were mainly in Danish, even though substantial parts have been translated into English. A new discussion of the Danish finds is thus imperative, particularly in a cultural, social and economic perspective.

It is evident that textiles, both in wool and linen, were very costly in Bronze Age civilisations (and later). We have probably overlooked the sheer value of the homespun Danish textiles and their economic power, and thus ignored the true importance of the work of women. The riches of the Danish Bronze Age and the original beauty of its artefacts have always been a puzzle, since the country and neighbouring areas are devoid of naturally found gold, tin and copper. It is likely that woollen textiles were the gold of the North and a main factor in the rise and workings of the Bronze Age everywhere. Both regionally and internationally, textiles were a motor of Bronze Age economics, providing peripheries with the means of obtaining materials – like metal – from the centres. Nevertheless, virtually all Bronze Age studies on exchange concentrate on metals and a few other categories (Clark 2009).

These new perspectives will, I hope, give rise to debates within and beyond the science of archaeology.

2

Dressing the North

2.1 Introduction

She dons the garb of a warrior,
She places a dagger in her girdle,
A poignard she places in her belt;
And on top she dons the garb of a woman.

Ugaric Poem of Aqht (Margalit 1981)

Woollen dresses from the Early Bronze Age, both male and female, have been found completely preserved in Denmark (see the figures; Table 1). The reason for the marvellously high degree of preservation of ancient organic materials is the famous split, hollowed and (after the deposition of the dressed dead body and accompanying artefacts) carefully closed coffins of mighty oak trunks. The coffins were covered by turf, forming a small barrow-like core in what was later to become a large burial mound. Before completing the mounds the cores were watered, which started a fast chemical process that created a crust of iron oxides surrounding the cores on all sides, leaving the turf around the coffin both completely drenched and starved of oxygen – as in a bog (Boye 1896; Broholm & Hald 1929-35; 1939; Hald 1980; Thomsen 1929-35; cf. Aner & Kersten 1973ff.; Randsborg & Christensen 2006; for textile fragments Bender Jørgensen 1986, in particular 15f.; cf. 133f.; 1992; for the preservation, Breuning-Madsen & Holst 1992-93). Incidentally, had linen textiles been present in the oak-coffins, these would also have been preserved; the conclusion therefore is that flax was most probably not used for cloth in the Nordic Early Bronze Age.

There are also complete garments from the Iron Age, but these are not always connected with particular individuals, and if they are, the context is different, since these dresses were found in bogs (van der Sanden 1996; Mannering, Gleba, Possnert & Heincmeier 2009). It is only in the case of the Early Bronze Age oak-coffin graves that we have full information on the solemn burial and religious and social manifestations concerning a high-ranking dead personage.

As appears from the following, much new evidence can be obtained from these extraordinary finds. Nevertheless, a fresh detailed and methodologically inventive first-hand study of the Bronze Age textiles is also needed, since what appears below is based mainly on already published evidence supplied by inspection of the finds.

Most of the oak-coffin finds are so well known – even internationally – that persons, dress and equipment from localities such as the following immediately come to mind (cf. Tables 5-7, etc.): Egtved – young woman with blouse and short string skirt; Skrydstrup – a finely coiffured young woman with blouse, wrap and other fine garments; Borum Eshøj – an old man with loincloth, cloak, and war cap; a young man with loincloth and cloak; and an old woman with blouse, wrap and other garments; Muldbjerg – a man with coat, cloak and war cap; Trindhøj – a man with coat, cloak, war cap, etc. Another fine war cap comes from Arildshøj (Schlabow c1974, cf. Tidow 1992). It is often felt that further introduction is unnecessary (cf. the references above). It should be borne in mind that other oak-coffin graves – like Guldhøj – have also yielded items of clothing, though not full garments, due to unprofessional excavation in the nineteenth century and sometimes less than perfect conditions of preservation (cf. Boye 1896).

A general, almost classical perspective on ancient dress was given by P.J. Riis, observing dress based on the shape of skins and woven garments of rectangular shape. He stressed the role of climate and put emphasis on particular cultural traditions and areas (Riis 1993; cf. Barber 1991; Jenkins 2002; even Gleba 2008). One of Riis's approaches followed the notion of animal hide prototypes for various garments from Classical Antiquity. Such ideas were also taken up by the perceptive M. Hald, who saw that the poncho-like pattern of the lovely woollen female blouses (or T-shirts) of the Bronze Age was modelled on a cut from a roe stag skin (Hald 1980, 344f.) (Fig. 1). This being the case, a long tradition for Nordic Bronze Age fashion could be argued, but not necessarily for its wool and weaving industries.

The oak-coffin dead rest on cow hides, never on furs of wild animals. The occasional suggestion of an Early Bronze Age trade in fine northern furs for Central Europe and the south of Europe finds no support in these graves. The dresses of the dead are all in wool, the cloth being a simply woven tabby, however elegantly cut. Woollen twills begin to appear in Central Europe around only 1000 BC and are not common in the North until the Iron Age.

So-called 'fulling', or stamping, carried out to soften the material, is common with the Early Bronze Age textiles, and there are often elaborate details, especially for the women, such as fine hair nets (in so-called sprang technique) and bonnets, professionally made embroidery, lovely tassels on fine belts, and, of course, the string skirts are very elegantly produced too (Figs 1-6). Sometimes they are decorated with bronze tubes in rows, making it possible to identify such skirts even when the organic material is long gone.

Stamping has often made the cloth look a bit wry and less competently made, which is incorrent. The technique also covers up the fact that the garments were often made of both large and small pieces of cloth, including repairs. In fact, stamping has made the fabric look and feel a little like felt. Carefully sewn-on shaggy pile was applied on cloaks, war caps and other textiles, possibly to imitate fine fur or cattle hides, even though woollen textiles would seem to be the more prestigious garments. It is likely that traditional garments in fur cast long and conservative shadows, as suggested by the patterns, but a

15

desire to add 'extras' is evident throughout; thus shaggy pile may be considered in line with embroidery and other secondary efforts. At any rate, these talents for stitching were no doubt honed through millennia of making garments from skin and fur.

With stamping mastered, it is strange that no attempts were seemingly made to produce felt cloth, ideal for caps, cloaks and mats (cf. Barber 1991, 215ff.). Such textiles would also have been much easier to produce than woven ones, however elegant the latter.

Dyes are seemingly unknown, but natural dyes may be difficult to document today due to heavy discolouring ('browning') in the water-logged oak-coffins. Modern techniques have revealed dyed Iron Age textiles (Mannering 2009, 101f.; van den Berghe, Gleba & Mannering 2009). Indeed, from Roswinkel in north-eastern Netherlands comes a woollen belt contemporary with Period II in the North; this belt is clearly coloured red (Schlabow 1974, 207f.). Four textile samples from the salt works of Middle Bronze Age Hallstatt in Austria (contemporary with Period II in the North) have demonstrated use of blue, yellow and red colours (Grömer 2006, 39).

Linen (flax) appears only in the Iron Age, and is mainly late. In Central Europe, linen was already common in the Neolithic, and almost no woollen textiles are known (Bender Jørgensen 1992, 114f.). Even in the Bronze Age, linen is rather more common on the European Continent than wool, to judge from the small fragments found. Perhaps the warmer wool is a northern, eastern, and south-eastern speciality, including Greece, while the cooler linen was preferred in the western climes, along with hides and furs (Bender Jørgensen 1992, 117 Fig. 140).

However, different conditions of preservation, which must always be taken into consideration, have the final word. If wood (a plant fibre) is present in a find and linen not, we can conclude that there was no linen (cf. the oak-coffin graves with woollen textiles), but wool may well have been present in finds and areas where only linen is preserved. One must bear in mind that distribution maps of organic materials are often inaccurate, being highly dependent on preservation. At any rate, spindle-whorls and loom-weights for wool occur in the Copper Age in Bulgaria (fifth millennium BC), for instance, and even as early as the Early Neolithic in the same region (Merkyte 2005, 108f.).

2.2. Technology

The archaeological age of the textile industry in Denmark is uncertain, but Early Bronze Age weaving techniques are not particularly advanced. In Europe weaving of textiles was already known several thousand years earlier, as indicated by the fortunate finds of linen textiles from the Neolithic in Switzerland (Vogt 1937; Drack 1969; Stöckli, Niffeler & Gross-Klee 1995).

A ceramic Neolithic spindle-whorl of the late fourth millennium BC with stamped patterns which may depict a loom is known from Denmark, but this a unique find (Lomborg 1975). Spindle-whorls are rare in Denmark before the early Iron Age; the earliest is possibly a specimen from the close of the Late Bronze Age, or Period VI (Broholm & Hald 1929-35, 295f., cf. Fig. 96; DB III, Grave 1399). Neolithic and Bronze Age spindle-whorls must otherwise have been in organic materials. An antler item which, judging by size and shape, might be a spindle-whorl, comes from an Early Bronze Age grave of Period II (Boye 1896, 21f. with Pl. II:A4; AK X;4856). The identification as a spindle-whorl is uncertain, in particular since it was in a rich male grave; the artefact might also be a knob for a chariot stick (Kaul & Randsborg 2008), or even from more recent times, perhaps part of a smoking pipe.

Spindle-whorls in organic materials were not included in the famous oak-coffin graves of the Early Bronze Age, which preserve such materials very well. The tools used for spinning the yarn of Bronze Age cloth are thus unknown, as are the looms. A couple of possible weaving tablets and other related tools date to the Neolithic (Madsen 1868, 17f. & Pl. 17:13; Glob 1952, nos 283, 611, and perhaps 610; cf. Broholm & Hald 1929-35, 320).

A single loom-weight comes from the mantle of a burial mound of the Late Middle Neolithic (early third millennium BC) in Jylland (Jutland), and is likely of the same period (Glob 1944, 247f., with Fig. 134). A grave find from north-western-most Germany, with a fragment of a woollen textile, is of the early Late Neolithic, and certainly dated to well before 2000 BC (Bender Jørgensen 1992, 114f.). A contemporary settlement find from Jylland (Jutland) holds loom-weights, a certain indicator of a textile technology comprising the upright warp-weighted loom, likely for wool (Rindel 1993, 20f.). In the cited case the weights occur with Continental Bell Beaker Culture elements. A grave from Jylland (Jutland) dated to the early Late Neolithic holds a fragment of a loom-weight; other loom-weights come from several Late Neolithic settlements in Jylland (Jutland) (cf. Davidsen 1982; Sarauw 2006, 39 Fig. 60), for instance Myrhøj, with Bell Beaker Culture impact in ceramics. Loom-weights are also found in the eastern regions of Denmark, for instance on Bornholm, in Late Neolithic settlements.

It is significant that dress pins (of bone or metal) occur frequently in the Late Neolithic period, and fibulae of bronze from Early Bronze Age Period II onwards (cf. Ebbesen 1995a). No doubt these items reflect the start of a common use of woollen textiles of some size, even though the bone pins often imitate metal ones and thus tell more about the presence of foreign metal than textiles. In the Nordic Late Bronze Age large fibulae were used by women as a decorative high status piece of jewellery, while pins once more became common (Baudou 1960, 118f.). The massive re-introduction of pins may reflect a change in garments otherwise unknown due to the custom of cremation.

An Early Bronze Age grave from Arnitlund in South Jylland (Jutland) held a simple dagger and one loom-weight (AK VII, 3563;A). (Confusion may exist with DB I, Grave 1109; cf. Broholm & Hald 1929-35, 300, with Fig. 104.) Early Bronze Age settlements have also yielded loom-weights (Boas 1983, 92f.; 99 Fig. 11), including the site of a Period II burial mound at Særslev, Sjælland (Zealand) (AK II, Grave 1008). A Late

Bronze Age settlement at Jegstrup, Northern Jylland (Jutland), likely of Period V, has revealed a single loom-weight (Davidsen 1982). Thus loom-weights of baked clay concentrate in the Late Neolithic and earliest Bronze Age, which includes the prime period of preserved textiles from the oak-coffin graves.

The character of the loom is much discussed. Upright warp-weighted looms appear long before 2000 BC in the southern and eastern parts of Europe (Barber 1991, 252 Fig. 13.2). Its existence in Denmark is inferred from the abovementioned finds of loom-weights from the Late Neolithic onwards. In-situ weights of a Late Bronze Age (Period IV) warp-weighted loom come from a settlement at Wallwitz near Burg in the northern part of Central Europe, but not quite the Bronze Age North (Stahlofen 1978) (Fig. 7). Otherwise we have to rely considerably on guesswork, including the existence of other types of loom, in particular the quite simple upright tubular variant (Hald 1980, 210f.).

A simple warp-weighted loom from Færøerne (Faeroe Islands), likely from around 1700 AD, is depicted in Fig. 8, which gives an idea of the attributes of such an instrument. A warp-weighted loom has only one beam (which may be fitted for rolling up the textile if a length longer than the height of the loom is required). It will produce cloth of various widths and lengths and in different qualities according to its size, various technical matters, the types of yarn used, its preparation, etc. For comparison, a simple upright tubular loom of the nineteenth century from the North-west Coast Indians is rendered in Fig. 9.

On the basis of the finds of Bronze Age textiles in Denmark, the looms had to accommodate the production of textiles up to two metres in width and four metres in length, likely involving several weavers, even three to four or more at the same time (cf. Broholm & Hald 1929-35, 242, cf. Fig. 41). To uncover an intact Early Bronze Age loom is an unrealistic dream, and looms do not appear on rock-carvings. The loom-like pattern on the stone with rock carvings from Storhøj at Fuglsang in Jylland (Jutland), a Bronze Age barrow, is in a different technique (metal chisel?) from other Bronze Age rock carvings and may be later (Glob 1969, 107 Fig. 115; 242f. No. 90). Thus suggestions can be made only on the basis of the textiles themselves.

The existence of a warp-weighted loom is traditionally indicated by (upper) starting borders or heading bands; such borders are common in Early Bronze Age textiles, including the fine white frilled blanket of the male Trindhøj grave of Period II (184x133/109 cm) and the blanket from Arildshøj (cf. Table 7). However, a number of 'weft repairs' observed on large textiles challenges the hypothesis. Such repairs occur typically when the warp is slack, which is normally not the case with a warp-weighted loom, but does occur on a tubular one (Alexandersen, Bennike, Hvass & Stærmose Nielsen 1981, 43f.; cf. Broholm & Hald 1939, 83f., already countering this argument; Broholm & Hald 1940, 127f. & 134f.; Bender Jørgensen 1986, 137f.; 1992, 118f.). Regarding the large wrap from Egtved, where the narrow end has a 'starting border', it has been argued that this is in fact a finishing border (Hald 1980, 158f.) (Fig. 17). An analysis of the Trindhøj blanket highlights the same uncertainty as to the type of loom (Broholm & Hald 1939, 73f.).

Perhaps some of these problems might be solved by suggesting a warp-weighted loom where the warp-ends are tied around, and weighed down, by a horizontal beam (like the lower one on a tubular loom, but lighter). The latter may even have been fastened to the uprights of the loom. Such a loom would not have loom-weights. The upright tubular loom with two beams, incidentally common in Ancient Egypt, has no loom-weights of course; it will, by definition, produce a length of cloth no longer than double the height of the loom, or rather less (cf. Bender Jørgensen 1992, 120f., cf. Fig. 164; generally, Barber 1991, 113f.) (cf. Fig. 9). This may not have been enough when we consider the longest textiles of the Early Bronze Age and the necessity of a practical working posture.

The argument for the tubular loom rests simply on the scarcity of loom-weights. It should be remembered, though, that loom-weights need not be made from baked clay; dried clay will suffice as will organic and other materials. As a consequence, the upright warp-weighted loom can be difficult to document on the basis of ordinary settlement finds.

The same is the case with the simple ground-loom, also with no loom-weights, which may have been used in Denmark earlier than the Late Neolithic, even though ground dampness and cold in the North would seem to prohibited it (Barber 1991, 83f.). This loom was common in Egypt before the New Kingdom.

Fine for making braids and belts, simple tablet weave produces long narrow pieces of cloth that can be stitched together for larger garments, such as the traditional almost 2x2 m Kente 'toga' of the Ashanti nation of Ghana (cf. Table 8; cf. Hald 1930; 1980, 225f.). Kente patterns even resemble decoration on the pottery of the late fourth millennium BC in Denmark (Glob 1952, 193-94; plus other Early Middle Neolithic products).

Regional aspects should also be borne in mind. In the Early Iron Age, loom-weights concentrate in south-western Denmark and northern Germany (Bender Jørgensen 1986, 136f.; 1992, 120f.). These areas have a particular preference for Z-spinning of yarn. In other areas, for instance North Jylland (Jutland) and Sjælland (Zealand), an advanced tubular loom may have been used; here S-spinning is common. Whether such observations can be applied to the Bronze Age is uncertain.

The width and length of the woven textiles are perhaps a better clue to the types of loom in use; at least such measures would be an indicator the size of the looms. Early Bronze Age measurement units are known from a yardstick found at Borum Eshøj indicating a foot of about 31 cm, which is very close to the Old Danish foot of 31.4 cm (Boye 1896, 53, figure). It appears from Figs 20-21, and the Tables, that female garments were about 1.20-1.25 m (4 feet) wide, except for the large wrap garment from the Egtved grave, which is nearly 2 m wide, or 6 feet. The latter is also quite long, more than 2.50 m, or about 8 feet. Other garments of the 4-foot standard width are either rather short, about $5\frac{1}{2}$ feet long (long plain skirts); or very long: one is $10\frac{1}{2}$ feet long, another $12\frac{1}{2}$ feet; both are wraps.

The male garments need a particular note since the kidney-shaped cloaks are cut from a rather wide piece of cloth of which the remaining parts may make up a coat with a strap over the one shoulder (Figs 11-12). The reconstructed width of this cloth is about 5 feet. Oval cloaks are made of cloth about 3½ feet wide. Loincloths are cut from products about 4 feet wide. One blanket is 4 feet wide – the standard width – another, a blanket from Muldbjerg, is about 7 feet wide.

Thus we have widths of cloths of respectively 3½ feet, 4 feet, 5 feet, 6 feet, and 7 feet. The small widths of 3½ and 4 feet are the most common. On principle, all products could have been made on the same loom, but for practical reasons this is unlikely. The loom from around 1700 AD in Fig. 9 accommodates a maximum width of cloth of about 5 feet; as shown, it is rigged for only 2½ feet. Since the great widths are less common, it would seem practical to operate with a minimum of two loom sizes, one for cloth up to 4 feet wide, and another for cloth double this width or more. The smaller looms could be operated by one or two weavers, the larger ones by double that number.

The famous Early Bronze Age grave from Kivig (Kivik), Skåne (Scania) carries rock-carving images on the inner side of the eight slabs of the long sides of the cist (Randsborg 1993, 33 Fig. 13) (Fig. 26). The images are framed, which would suggest that we are dealing with stone editions of embroidered tapestries. The frames are almost square and rather small, about 75 cm high, a couple probably about 90 cm, which would correspond to cloth widths of 3 and 3½ feet respectively. A cloth width of 4 feet is suggested by the textile-like Late Neolithic or Bronze Age images on the huge slate capstone of several cists in Mjeltehaugen, Norway (Randsborg 1993, 72f. with Figs 38a-b; reconstruction by Linge 2005); the length of this 'textile' is about 8 feet.

At Zedau in northernmost Central Germany, a Late Bronze Age settlement of Period IV, an excavated line of loom-weights was found to be 0.59 m long, or only 2 feet; however, the weights were found in what appears to be a large posthole, one of four, of a small structure about 4x4 m, perhaps a weaving hut with a slightly lowered floor (Horst 1985, 105). A better preserved find comes from the settlement at Wallwitz near Burg in the same general area (Stahlhofen 1978). A well-documented line of loom-weights is up to 2.5 m long, reflecting the production of cloth 8 feet wide, or as wide as the widest known Early Bronze Age textiles from the North. The find is dated to Period IV of the Late Bronze Age; it consists of a shallow pit or work area between two postholes for the loom uprights (Fig. 7).

Another issue is the length of the textiles, which varies from 2½ feet for male loincloths to 12½ feet for the longest female wrap. Male kidney shaped cloaks are 7½ to 8 feet long, oval cloaks are about 6 feet long. Garments of 5 feet or more in length (including the blanket fragment from Arildshøj of more than 4½ feet) must have been rolled up on the beam of a warp-weighted loom or produced on a tubular loom, even though it seems unlikely that the latter could be more than 6 feet tall (nearly 2 m) and still function effectively, i.e. with no slack warp threads.

A warp-weighted loom for relatively narrow and relatively short textiles could thus have been a simple solution for many households. But the larger textiles call for other solutions and certainly for larger looms. Still, we may have underestimated the character of the Early Bronze Age textile-production in the North, which may have been more centralised and more professional in organisation than usually imagined. The standardised cloth sizes, given above in Bronze Age feet, give us cause for such speculation, as does the centralised production of many fine gold and bronze items from the same social environment. Even though the North had no palaces on the Aegean model, organisation of production was elaborate.

2.3 Cloth

Acquisition of wool and production of textiles are described in detail in Linear B texts from Late Bronze Age Greece (Ventris & Chadwick 1956). The northern Early Bronze Age produced no palaces, of course, but other factors were probably similar in these two dynamic regions. Thus it is reasonable to believe that no substantial differences existed between the Early Bronze Age in the North and the contemporary Aegean palaces with respect to textile production and the role of cloth in exchange and otherwise. At least, the elements were throughout the same.

The quotations from Linear B tables given below, and arranged in an appropriate sequence, follow closely the entire process of the woollen industry, from animal to product as guided by appropriate specialists. Making of cloth is women's work in the Aegean; interestingly, both women and men might be tailors.

Linear B tablets of the Late Bronze Age from the Palace of Knossos
Tablet 71. *Ka-te-u* [personal name]: at Ku-tato, 100 rams; 40 kg of wool; deficit 35 kg of wool.
Tablet 74. So much sheep's wool from Phaistos [palace]: 1368 kg.

Linear B tablets of the Late Bronze Age from the Palace of Pylos
Tablet 3. Four sons of the carders, three boys.
Tablet 4. Twenty-one spinning-women, twenty-five girls, four boys: one *ta-*.
Tablet 15. At Pylos: five sons of the Ti-nwa-sian [ethnic group] weavers (sons of rowers at *A-pu-ne-we* [place-name]), two boys.
Tablet 52. ...

so-rope-o [ethnic adjective] tailors	[MEN[1] nn]
ko-ri-si-jo [ethnic adjective] tailors	[MEN nn]
ka-ro-ke-e [ethnic adjective] tailors	[MEN nn]
ra-ni-jo-ne [ethnic adjective] tailors	MEN [nn]
[ ]-*ka-si-da* [ethnic adjective] tailors	MEN 20[

Tablet 115. The private plot of R., so much seed: 180 l. wheat.
Now this is how the tenants hold plots belonging to R.:
P., the king's fuller, holds a lease, so much seed: 12 l. wheat,
...

Linear B tablets of the Late Bronze Age from the Palace of Knossos
Tablet 209. From *Se-to-i-ja* [place-name]:
Forty edged cloths of royal type, 200+ measures of wool;
Three cloths of *tu-na-mo* type, several hundred [?] measures of wool.[2]
Tablet 211. [?]: Sixteen cloaks of *ko-u-ra* type, 26⅔ measures of wool;
One cloth of *tu-na-mo* type, three measures of wool;
Four edged cloths, twenty-six measures of wool.

2. Dressing the North

Tablet 213. Thus Areios received delivery from outside [the palace], and
there are not ...:
From Phaistos: Two clean edged cloths, fourteen dirty edged
cloths,
...

Tablet 214. Twenty-five cloaks with white edge suitable for followers,
provided with *pe-ne-* [grease?], of better quality; and one
bundle.

Tablet 215. Thirty-five cloaks with white edge suitable for guest-gifts, with
red [something]; and one bundle.

Tablet 218. ... of [ ]-*tās* [male name]: one cloth with coloured edge,
thirty-seven cloths with white edge,
two dyed cloths.
So many in all: forty cloths.
Deficit: six cloths.

Tablet 221. [Garments:] [x] clean cloths of *nu-wa-ja* type,
seventeen dirty cloths, three tunics,
one cloth of *nu-wa-ja* type, torn and mended,
one ... cloth.

Tablet 222. Fine linen, of the tribute: a tunic = 1 kg. of bronze[3] ...
A *sa-pa* [name of a textile] = 45 g. [of bronze],
over-shirt[s] = 1 kg. of bronze ...

Tablet 225. *Do-ti-ja* [place-name]: 54 kg. of wool, makes three cloths.
The *ka-ma* [agricultural holding]: 36 kg. of wool, makes two
cloths.
Sa-mu?-ta-jo [personal name]: 72 kg of wool, makes four
cloths.

[1] Symbol for a man; female tailors also occur (cf. Ventris & Chadwick 1956,
123 & 407 right column, *ra-pi-ti-ra*, etc.).

[2] One measure of wool equals 3 kg., or the amount from four sheep (Ventris
& Chadwick 1956, 57).

[3] The bronze measures are most likely indicators of value, in fact prices.

That a linen industry was also present in the Aegean appears from a smaller number of Linear B texts, including
tablets from Pylos (Tablet no. 8) and Knossos (Tablet no. 219)
(Ventris & Chadwick 1956, 295f.):

Tablet 8.   *At Eudeiwelos: four sons of the flax-workers.*
Tablet 219.   *Linen cloth from [Da]-te-we-ja: one cloak, one tunic.*

A highly important element in woollen textile production is
the particular breeds of sheep available, and when. Nordic

Early Bronze Age cloth is characterised by homogeneous wool, which ought to reflect organised sheep ranching, though this does not exclude some trade in wools, as well as in finished cloth and garments. Early Bronze Age trade in textiles is evident from a silk (likely wild) found in a Period III grave from northernmost Germany (Schmidt 2004; 2007; Scherping & Schmidt 2007; Randsborg & Christensen 2006, 25f.). The previously mentioned unusually wide wrap from the famous Egtved grave of a young woman from Early Bronze Age Period II may also represent an import due to its great width (Broholm & Hald 1929-35, 281 Fig. 114; Alexandersen, Bennike, Hvass & Stærmose Nielsen 1981, 37f. with 38 Fig. 11) (Fig. 17). The same is the case for the very wide but also rather short blanket from the equally famous male Muldbjerg grave of the same period (Broholm & Hald 1929-35, 224f. with 229 Fig. 15). Some of the fine textiles from Lille Dragshøj, Jylland (Jutland), might also be imports, including pieces with elaborate borders (Broholm & Hald 1929-35, 247f. with Figs 36 & 37:2; Boye 1896, Pl. XXIII shows larger pieces of this garment) (cf. Table 2). However, in all cases the weave is rather ordinary, which would argue against these textiles being imports.

Long-distance bulk trade in wool is not unlikely, wool being a product that societies in Norway and Sweden were capable of producing in sufficient qualities and for which exotic gold and bronze might have been acquired from Denmark by ship. Export of quality wool from the Baltic islands of Gotland or the much nearer Öland is not wholly unlikely, and western Denmark was always a great producer of wool, while the islands may have concentrated on animals other than sheep (Randsborg 1980, 54f.; 1985, 236f., cf. 239 Fig. 11.4, Öland & Gotland). The island of Bornholm in the Baltic (less than 600 km^2) is known to have had between 25,000 and 30,000 sheep of a breed producing very fine wool in the pre-industrial early nineteenth century. Export of wool is not recorded for Bornholm in this period, probably due to the increasing import of English industrial cloth from around 1800 onwards. The area of Thy, Northwest Jylland (Jutland), with close contacts to south-western Norway, is very rich indeed in Early Bronze Age graves. At the end of the eighteenth century each of the manor houses of Thy owned 150-200 sheep, and smallholders 8-10 (Aagaard 1802). A young sheep would yield 1-1½ pounds of wool annually, a three-year-old twice as much.

A novel technology in the Late Bronze Age is cloth made from nettles (Køie 1943). Nettle textiles appear in a princely grave from Voldtofte on Fyn (Funen) with rich imports and golden objects (of Period V), so an imported nettle textile cannot be excluded (cf. Thrane 1984). The very first twill in Denmark, perhaps also an import, was found on a female bog body from Borremose in North Jylland (Jutland); the find dates to the Late Bronze Age (ninth century BC), according to a C-14 date (Hald 1980, 20f.). Another early twill is from the end of the Late Bronze Age (Period VI), found in an unusually richly furnished grave from Håstrup on Fyn (Funen); this grave also held imports including a rare composite glass bead, likely Phoenician in origin (Thrane 2004, (1) 243f.; (2) Pl. 76:1-14). Twill requires a complex loom, no doubt a novelty at that time in Denmark (cf. Bender Jørgensen 1986, 17f.).

It is unfortunate that fully preserved Early Bronze Age textiles come only from Jylland (Jutland), small fragments being the only textiles from the rich and productive cultural environments of Sjælland (Zealand) and Northern Germany. Comparative materials might have solved the riddle of the very wide textiles from Egtved and Muldbjerg, and the elaborate borders of Lille Dragshøj. In fact, according to reports dating from between the twelfth and the early nineteenth century, oak-coffins with preserved textiles are known to have been found on Sjælland (Zealand), but only bronzes have survived from these early excavations (cf. Randsborg & Christensen 2006, 3f.).

Future stable isotope studies of wool and in particular of cloth will no doubt provide further evidence of travel of, even trade in, wool and textiles (for the methodology, cf. Frei, Frei, Mannering, Gleba, Nosch & Lyngstrøm 2009; cf. Frei, Skals, Gleba & Lyngstrøm 2009). A requirement is of course that wools, soil-types etc. not only from Denmark but also from neighbouring and even more remote regions are taken up for scrutiny, preferably in a temporal perspective.

Cloth was no doubt very costly in the Nordic Early Bronze Age: smaller pieces of material were used to finish larger items. Much work and talent were put into tailoring, secondary stitching, and the common fulling (stamping) (generally, see Barber 1991). Cloth was also costly in the Aegean (cf. Linear B Tablet 222 above): a larger garment being the equivalent of 1 kg of bronze, a fortune in the North. The textile industry was highly important everywhere.

Spinning in the Nordic Early Bronze Age is always of a single thread; spinning of several threads together only comes later. A seemingly unimportant detail like the direction of spinning changes somewhat over time (Bender Jørgensen, Munksgaard & Stærmose Nielsen 1982, 45f.; Bender Jørgensen 1986, 16f., including textile fragments). In Period II more than 70% of the textiles belong to the S/Z group – S and Z signalling the two directions of spinning of the warp and the weft respectively – while about 15% belong to the S/S group. In Period III only about 35% belong to the S/Z group, while the S/S group has grown to more than 50% – percentages which also hold true for the Late Bronze Age; the S/S group disappears only in the Early Iron Age, around 100 AD.

S/S spinning is common in the Early Iron Age in North Jylland (Jutland), with textiles of the so-called Huldremose group made on a tubular loom; Z/Z spinning, by contrast, occurs in South Jylland/North Germany with the Haraldskjær textiles made on a warp-weighted loom (Bender Jørgensen 1986, 26f.; 1992, 120f.). Going back to the very wide Early Bronze Age textiles, the wrap and the blanket from Egtved and Muldbjerg respectively (cf. above) are both of the usual S/Z spinning composition, incidentally the same as the fine white blanket from Trindhøj (Broholm & Hald 1929-35, 130, etc.). The spinning directions of all the well preserved Early Bronze Age textiles are given in Table 4. As expected from the fragments, S/Z is dominant in Period II; S/S weaves appear in

Period III. Among the deviating garments are the cloak and some other items from Guldhøj, produced in S/S spinning, and the cloak of the old man in Borum Eshøj, also in S/S.

Since S/S is almost only known in southern and western Jylland (Jutland) in Period II, while it occurs across the country in Period III, the phenomenon should be seen in connection with the general expansion of Period III norms from west to east, perhaps accompanied by a loom of the tubular variety, if we rely on the Early Iron Age findings (cf. Randsborg 1968). The changing modes of spinning find no functional explanation in terms of textile character or quality, but using only one type of yarn may have simplified and standardised the production a little (cf. Bender Jørgensen 1986, 25). The shift represents what might be termed the 'unconscious' in society (and archaeology), in fact different traditions of learning which result in almost invisible cultural differences, usually overlooked or ignored: the very minimum level of cultural and behavioural distinction.

The quality of cloth of most of the preserved Early Bronze Age garments from the oak-coffin graves of Central and Southern Jylland (Jutland) are presented in Table 2. It is noted that there are no differences between genders. However, dress items worn close to the body, like loin-cloths, T-shirts (blouses), and in particular foot-wrappings (socks), may be of finer materials than other garments; the same seems to be true of sheets and blankets.

Furthermore, there seem to be no regional differences in cloth quality as measured by numbers of warp threads per cm, though cloth finer than the garments preserved in the oak-coffin graves has also been recorded (data extracted from Bender Jørgensen 1986, 185ff.: the catalogue; cf. Bender Jørgensen 1992). Such exquisite textiles several with more than 10 warp threads per cm – have only been studied as small cloth fragments preserved by metal salts on corroding bronzes, not as anything like garments that can be reconstructed, even partly. While the full garments are highly important, the very many metal-soaked fragments of textiles provide a rather more general picture.

Textiles were also getting finer over time, as measured by a higher number of warp threads per cm (Randsborg & Christensen 2006, 24 Fig. 11) (Table 3). In Period II, two-thirds of the cloth has 5 or fewer threads per cm and only about a quarter has 6-10 threads per cm. In Period III, both the pieces that have 1-5 and those that have 6-10 threads per cm make up nearly half of the material. In both periods less than 10% of the cloth has more than 10 threads per cm. There are examples of fine gold threads being wound around woollen ones for decoration (e.g. Kersten 1936, Taf. XXII:18; Broholm 1943-49/I Grave 1896). In the Late Bronze Age, the material is much more limited (due to cremation practices which had already begun in Period III). It would seem that both the coarse group and the finest one make up nearly half the material, but the high percentage of very fine textiles is mainly the result of finds in a couple of princely graves from Period V at Voldtofte, Fyn (Funen) (Thrane 1984).

In conclusion, details demonstrate the existence of professional groups of shepherds, wool-makers, weavers and needlewomen, in much the same way as the production of fine bronze and gold items – the other grave goods – required skilled, sometimes even highly skilled, craftsmen. Certainly, the wool was of different types, though all was of even quality, and weaving differed in both quality and type. Thus there was ample room for exchange of both raw materials and finished products. Dress design is throughout simple and elegant, even aristocratic. Garments like the men's cloaks are cut to shape, and women's blouses or T-shirts composed of several pieces of cloth in fulfilment of both functional and aesthetic requirements.

In fact, there is a correspondence between the simple aesthetics of the textiles and the fine bronzes, even though the latter are complex and decorated; the former hardly so. Textile elements may well lie behind some of the features of the the bronzes, like the thin twisted bows of fibulae and much of the decoration, for instance in the form of ribbons or fields of small triangles and other microelements imitating weave. The bronzes were densely decorated with geometrical motifs that changed constantly over time, providing us with an archaeological chronology. Golden objects, characteristically difficult to date for archaeologists, are by contrast rather simple and simply decorated, gold belonging to the unchanging world of deities and supernatural powers.

Such rationale is supported by the naked body, which in the Bronze Age was also left without or with only very little decoration (cf. §3.5). It is likely that everything related to the human body, such as garments, or conceived as a body, such as pottery, was left undecorated.

2.4 Men

The oak-coffin graves represent the Early Bronze Age elite, as we can see from the large barrows and the burial goods in general. The diversity in grave goods and their arrangements are impressive and often difficult to explain, even though clear cultural patterns occur (Randsborg & Christensen 2006). The Early Bronze Age finds with completely preserved garments almost all date to Period II of the Early Bronze Age – basically, the fourteenth century BC. Although the famous Skrydstrup grave is of Period III according to a C-14 date (Bender Jørgensen, Munksgaard & Stærmose Nielsen 1982, 43f.) and such a date is somewhat supported by the golden earrings, the grave was found at the centre of the mound and should thus be primary; two, supposedly secondary, graves in the same mound held swords of Period II date: this calls for a new C-14 date. The other graves are all dendro-dated and/or archaeologically dated (Randsborg & Christensen 2006).

Male graves with full garments comprise Muldbjerg, Trindhøj, and the old and the young man from Borum Eshøj, but there are others, though not as well preserved (Table 7). The men appear clean shaven, in death at least (razors are often found with the grave goods). They wore their hair rather short and in different styles (Boye 1896, Pl. X;1; Jensen 1998, 94), including shaved temples, and 'cock's comb' (Boye 1896,

31

XXIII;2; Jensen 1998, 56). Pubic hair and hair in the armpits were not cut. Virtually nothing is known about cosmetics or tattoos, which may have been unknown, although there are prehistoric examples of the latter (cf. Dierck 1976 for uncertain finds). Small polished hematite stones have been found in male graves in a few cases, possibly used for producing red colour (Strömberg 1975, 30f.). It has been suggested that thin awls (in the Late Bronze Age sometimes very thin), found in graves, were used in tattooing (e.g. Stjernquist 1961, Pls XVII;7 & XXIII;2).

A long, narrow piece of cloth (c. 10x100 cm) from a male grave is perhaps a breechcloth (Boye 1896, 107f. & Pl. XXII:A1) (Table 9). The traditional suggestion that it is a belt is wrong, since male belts are very narrow, much longer, and produced using a different technique. A scarf is an option (though it is still quite narrow), as is a puttee (though it is rather short for that purpose). Close-fitting underwear has not been found in the oak-coffin graves, but a couple of identical male figurines with tall brimmed hats from a Period II deposit at Stokholt (Stockhult) in Skåne (Scania) are clad in short and likely closed loincloths, or rather in broad breechcloths (Randsborg 1993, 111f.; cf. Figs 60, 64 & 65). The figurines have Near Eastern prototypes.

The men wore belted coats or loincloths (trousers were un-known). Large kidney-shaped or oval cloaks, respectively about 2.5-3 m^2 and 2 m^2 in size, were worn over one shoulder to free an arm and a hand (Fig. 11). The kidney-shaped cloaks are more or less identical to the eighth-century BC cloaks from Verucchio in Central Italy, as well as to Roman military cloaks (Elis 2002; Gleba 2008, 49 Fig. 29; Hald 1980, 318 Fig. 1277, cf. Fig. 1278). A heavy war cap with fraying – many hundreds of short strings added on to the cap for visual effect – is common (cf. Schlabow *c.* 1974), perhaps a reference to fine caps of fur. In fact, such caps are really very thick woollen 'helmets'. In Trind-høj a softer pixie-cap for use day and night has been found. Foot-wrappings and leather sandals have also been found in the male oak-coffin graves; they are of the same type for both men and women and are discussed further below (§2.5).

2. Dressing the North

Men were often buried with weapons, including swords or daggers and sometimes fighting axes (the coffins usually had no room for lances, which are quite common in treasures). In Muldbjerg a flange-hilted sword was found, a fine fighting weapon, in Trindhøj a prestigious all-metal-hilted sword; both were likely imported from Central Europe. Jylland (Jutland), connected by land with the Continent, has produced many foreign artefacts. Indeed, the Early Bronze Age highways of Jylland are revealed clearly by intricate strings of thousands of large mounds: in ancient times no doubt carrying the names of the dead but to which we have been forced to assign modern place-names (e.g. Randsborg & Christensen 2006, 40 Fig. 20).

The male figurines with breechcloths from Stokholt, mentioned above, also wear tall hats with holes in the brim for decoration (Randsborg 1993, 111f.; cf. Figs 60, 64 & 65). The figurines were most likely made locally, but have movable arms; they copy Near Eastern prototypes (of deities or divine rulers). Nevertheless, they indicate knowledge in the North of other types of headgear than the war and pixie-caps. Tall hats were likely used in the cult. A male cult garment, in fact a narrow belted shirt, or T-shirt, with open flanks ending in two V-shaped tongues covering the crotch like a breechcloth is inferred from figurines and a textile fragment found in a grave at Hvidegården, Sjælland (Zealand) (Lomborg 1981) (cf. Fig. 22). The particular shape is difficult to explain; perhaps it harks back to a skinned animal hide. At any rate, it seems to mix female dress elements (the T-shirt) and the male cover of the abdomen, incidentally in a way that is rather revealing.

Men wore little jewellery, except for large buttons and bossed tutuli (in pairs) for the leather sword-belt worn over the shoulder. Such tutuli were tokens of rank, since they are found only in richly furnished graves. Occasionally, golden items occur, including bracelets; combs are common, as are purses with a razor and other toiletries, and tools, including strike-a-lights. Various fine drinking vessels accompany the well-to-do male 'cupbearers' (in metal, or in wood with costly nails of tin). Even folding stools, another token of rank, were included in the

33

burials, as well as pointed sticks to drive the chariot-horses (Kaul & Randsborg 2008).

The males radiated social and martial powers, including foreign contact: all copper, tin and gold were imported. Nevertheless, Denmark is the European area of this period that sees the highest amount of bronze and gold deposited in graves, which reflects a particular energy and high degree of social organisation, no doubt motivated by ideology and religion.

A mere 20% of the males hold 50% or more of the bronze in their graves, and nearly all the gold (Fig. 12). Translated into other resources, this is indeed a highly stratified society, not least because the graves in barrows belong to the elites. The consumption of textiles, based on selected well preserved male grave finds, is given in Table 10, revealing about 3-7 m^2 of cloth per grave, plus caps, belts etc. In contemporary Aegean and Near Eastern societies a large garment held the same value as 1 kg of bronze or thereabouts (Ventris & Chadwick 1956, 320f., Tablet no. 222, cf. Part V below). By such standards, the textiles in a Nordic Early Bronze Age grave would have been more costly than the bronzes, however valuable the latter as exotica in Scandinavia.

2.5 Women

Female graves that come immediately to mind are Skrydstrup, a young woman, Egtved, another young woman, and the old woman from Borum Eshøj (Tables 5-6). But there are more, although with less well preserved garments. In particular, the short string skirt at Egtved and the long wraps at Skrydstrup and Borum Eshøj have aroused discussion.

The women's hair was either worn rather short, i.e. medium length, or much longer and worn in a pony tail, or in fine, almost regal, tall coiffures (with hair pad and nets) (Fig. 1); the hair of the young Skrydstrup woman was ash-blonde and up to 60 cm long. As with men, pubic hair and hair in the armpits was not cut.

Hair nets have been found at Skrydstrup and Hvilshøj, bonnets at Skrydstrup and Borum Eshøj (the latter almost a thick hair net); elaborate tall coiffures are documented at

Skrydstrup and Hvilshøj (Lomborg 1963; 1964; cf. Bender Jørgensen, Munksgaard & Stærmose Nielsen 1982). Use of
cosmetics has never been demonstrated, nor have tattoos, but
small hematite stones for producing red colour also occur in
female graves (Thrane 1962).

Women wore open-necked blouses or 'T-shirts' with short
sleeves, in addition to various skirts: shorter string skirts as
well as long plain skirts (not previously acknowledged) (Fig. 18,
etc.). The blouses were made of one main piece of cloth and
various smaller additions. Women also wore very large and
often thick wraps (a term introduced here) of about 4.0-4.5 m^2
in size, to cover the head and body. Such garments have previously been designated 'heavy skirts', since they are wrapped
around the dead body from under the armpits to below the feet.
Both wraps and long plain skirts are rectangular in shape and
may also serve as blankets. A long plain skirt may even have
been used to carry a small child on the back in African fashion,
the cloth also serving as a napkin.

Underwear was not worn by either gender, to judge from the
oak-coffin graves (pubic hair is attached to the inner side of the
piece of garment worn around the hips); in fact, underwear for
women was not common in the Danish countryside a mere 150
years ago. However, it may also have been omitted in graves. It
is argued below that Bronze Age women used a napkin or a
breechcloth during menstruation, or for other reasons (§4.2).

Woollen belts are standard in the Early Bronze Age, female
ones being the finest and broadest; they also have large tassels
(Fig. 5). Both men and women may have worn fur or leather
garments (never found in the graves), or blankets (found in the
graves), as outer garments against the cold and rain (van der
Sanden 1996, 124 etc., incl. Figs 170, 173 & 205 for Dutch
Early Bronze Age specimens; Hald 1980, 18f.; 313f. for Danish
Late Bronze Age specimens of about 1.5 m^2 in size from Borre-
mose; cf. van der Sanden 1996, 194 etc.; Jensen 2002, 397f.) (cf.
Fig. 29). A net-bag was included in the female Borum grave (cf.
Boye 1896, Pl. XI:5); a similar, better preserved one is known
from a Late Bronze Age bog find of Period V (Broholm & Hald

Bronze Age Textiles

1929-35, 274f.; 292). With dresses without pockets such bags would have been a necessity, strangely overlooked up to now.

Various items of jewellery, including some earrings, necklaces and neck-collars, belt-plates (images of the sun), bracelets (but rarely ankle rings), common tutuli with a point, combs and a few other items complete the female appearance. Strike-a-lights never occur. Some senior women carried daggers, likely signalling their status as wives of 'swordsmen'. Bossed tutuli, common among senior men, are extremely rare in female graves and found only in richly furnished ones, likely indicating a relationship akin to the male sword-female dagger one. Drink also accompanied the women, but never the fine vessels of the male graves, which were likely for diplomacy and ceremonial symposia. Notably, the young but high-ranking Skrydstrup woman had no such vessel; perhaps drinks in female graves were a symbol of participation in the cult.

Thus, women radiate social position and reference to the cult of the sun: no doubt women participated actively in the cult. The amount of bronze invested in female graves is significantly less than in male ones, even though the dead were all members of the aristocracy (Fig. 13). There is only a little gold in female graves. But women were higher consumers of wealth in terms of cloth and dress items than the men (cf. Table 10). As burial gifts, the women were given textiles in an amount of almost 7 to almost 10 m², plus hair nets, bonnets, belts, etc., a high value indeed by Aegean and Near Eastern standards (cf. Ventris & Chadwick 1956, 320f., Tablet no. 222; and Part IV below). Interestingly, the investment in male and female graves may well have been more balanced than the metal artefacts would indicate (cf. Randsborg & Christensen 2006, 30f. Figs 12-14).

Late Bronze Age figurines and several rock-carvings depict young almost naked women – wearing only short string skirts and necklaces – engaged in acrobatic dances, no doubt in connection with cultic ceremonies (Broholm & Hald 1929-35, 322f.; 1939, 93f.; Djupedal & Broholm 1952) (Fig. 22). Since nearly all Late Bronze Age figurines, male included, wear necklaces, the status of these is uncertain: deities, priests, or other members

36

of a cult group? The necklaces may indicate that the persons in question are deities or initiated ('married') to a god. Very few Early Bronze Age figurines are known, none wearing necklaces despite this being a divine characteristic according to their Near Eastern prototypes (e.g. Randsborg 1993, 112 Fig. 150).

Foot-wrappings and leather sandals have also been found in female oak-coffin graves, including the exceptional Skrydstrup grave (Broholm & Hald 1939, 84f.; Hald 1972, 11f.). Leather is not preserved well in the acid environment of the oak-coffins, but the certain finds of leather sandals occur in graves that seem to denote very high rank (cf. Tables 5; 7; 10). In the Scandinavian Bronze Age rock-carvings both naked and, far more often, shod pairs of feet occur, the latter sometimes taking the shape of a wheel-cross as a result of tying strings across the arch of the foot (Randsborg 1993, 81f.).

The presence in both female and male graves of pieces of cloth wound (but not bound) around the shinbones, ankles, or feet is at first somewhat puzzling. These garments, of different size and shape, appear in the female Egtved and Skrydstrup graves, as well as in the male ones of Muldbjerg, Trindhøj and Borum Eshøj (the old man); these are likely to have functioned as some kind of 'socks' or 'stockings' (Thomsen 1929-35; Broholm & Hald 1939; Hald 1972, 14f.; 21f.; cf. Boye 1896) (Tables 5; 7; 10). The presence of wrappings indicates the use of some sort of footwear, not necessarily included in the coffin. An elaborate 'foot-wrapping' or sock was found in the male Guldhøj grave; this composite item has even been taken to be a mitten, or a shoe (Hald 1972, 16; 22f.; cf. Jensen 1998, 134f.).

Most of the foot-wrappings are long, roughly rectangular, and likely customised. In the Egtved grave there were four specimens, all long and triangular, likely made of discarded pieces of cloth, including remains from the making of an oval male cloak (Eskildsen & Lomborg 1977, 5: figure). Had it not been for their position in the grave (wound around the feet), at least one or two might have been taken for a breechcloth or napkin (cf. §4.2).

37

3

Analyses

3.1 String skirts

Elegant, intricately woven short string skirts were common in the Bronze Age, as revealed not only by the completely preserved textile specimen of the Egtved grave, measuring 154x38 cm unfolded, but also by various Late Bronze Age figurines (cf. Figs 22; 24). The strings of the skirts move almost freely and yet the lower part of the body is decently covered, since the skirt is wound at least twice around the body and the strings tied together above as well as below (Fig. 3).

Sheet metal bronze tubes, used in series for decorating the front of string skirts, have been found in a large number of Early Bronze Age graves, mainly of Period II, where, at most, only fragments of the textile have survived (Fig. 4; Tables 5-6). It seems that the length and the number of the tubes reflect status. Even Late Bronze Age graves may hold such tubes, as in the case of a cremation from Addit, Jylland (Jutland) (Sehested 1884, 127f.; 130; Pl. XXVI:4a-b: rather short wide tubes). The bronze tubes have augmented the number of known string skirts substantially; incidentally, they also appear in deposits.

A very large number of sheet metal bronze tubes for string skirts came to light in a colossal Period II deposit from Vognserup, Sjælland (Zealand) (Rieck 1971-72; AK 1043I; cf. Randsborg & Christensen 2006, 122f.). The find comprises thirty-four neck-collars, two large belt-plates (one with calendar properties), four small belt plates, two bossed tutuli, thirty-four tutuli with points, four spiral finger-rings, and almost two hundred tubes for string skirts: In other words, several sets of fine equipment probably for a senior leader (and her deputy?) plus other members of a cult group. The two prominent women were likely married (indicated by the neck-collars and bossed tutuli) (cf. Table 14). However, daggers are not present in the find (cf. below), possibly indicating that daggers were considered personal property and only included in graves. This observation may indicate a distinction between office and person.

A very large number of tubes for string skirts came to light in a very rich Period II deposit at Rye on Sjælland (AK 669; cf. Randsborg & Christensen 2006, 122). This find comprises three neck-collars, three belt plates (one with calendar properties), twenty-one tutuli with points, five or six spiral arm rings, seven or more spiral finger-rings, and two sickles: three sets of high-class equipment probably for senior members of cult groups; as above, the members were possibly married, but again the daggers were not included (cf. Table 14). Finally, in a deposit at Skagen, Jylland (Jutland) many tubes were found together with a neck-collar, a belt-plate, and six or more tutuli with points, plus other items (DB I, M57): another set of jewel-lery for a high-ranking woman, likely a member of a cult-group, and likely married; again the dagger is not included.

A deposit of sheet metal bronze tubes, rather short and quite wide, is of the Late Bronze Age (Period IV) and comes from Kirkendrup, Fyn (Funen) (DB III, M42). The find holds very rich female jewellery and other items, including two highly decorated so-called hanging vessels (for holding amulets), two very large tutuli, four fine bracelets and two spiral arm-rings: likely the equipment for two high-ranking female members of a cult-group. In addition, the find holds four plus one imported bronze drinking vessels, likely a male element. Similar bronze tubes were found with horse gear and a bracelet in a rich Late Bronze Age grave (Period V) from Bevtoft in South Jylland (Jutland) (DB III, 1372).

A mid-fourth millennium BC grave from Ettrup in North Jylland (Jutland) displays a short file of twelve equally long tube-shaped amber beads across the middle of the grave

(Brøndsted 1934, 156f., with Abb. 15). These may have been attached to a belt or, rather more likely, to a string skirt. A large number of similar beads but of varying length were found scattered in all directions at the one end of the grave, likely attached to a wrap covering the dead person, seemingly a woman. Long tube-shaped beads in amber (or copper) appear in contemporary pot deposits, perhaps of fine clothing (cf. Ebbesen 1995b). The point is that string skirts may go back a long way in time (cf. Gimbutas 1982, 44f. with Figs 1ff. for the Balkans).

In the grave of the young woman from Egtved were, apart from the famous – even notorious – short string skirt (notably without bronze tubes), a blouse or T-shirt (Fig. 3; Tables 5-6). The string skirt was wound twice around the body. It rested on the hips, the girth being 73 cm. The waist was only 60 cm, as indicated by the knotted ornamental tasselled belt (Thomsen 1929-35; cf. Alexandersen, Bennike, Hvass & Stærmose Nielsen 1981).

In the graves at Borum Eshøj (old woman) and Skrydstrup (young woman) blouses or T-shirts like the one in the Egtved grave were also found, but in the former graves the bodies were shrouded in a very large piece of cloth, the traditional 'heavy skirt', here termed 'wrap', for reasons elaborated below (Figs 15-17; Tables 5-6). Borum Eshøj and Skrydstrup do not contain string skirts, which of course has lent credibility to the suggestion that the shrouding wraps were in fact long skirts.

A very large garment such as the wrap, which is in fact toga-sized, is very difficult to wear without it being carried over one or both shoulders (and/or the head) (Boye 1896; Broholm & Hald 1929-35; Randsborg & Christensen 2006). Worn folded under the armpits, it would simply inhibit movement. Certainly, the rather weak woollen belts found in the two graves cannot have held up a large heavy wrap during daily and ceremonial chores (cf. Fig. 14). Nevertheless, it was exactly such a woollen belt that was wound not only around the large wrap in the Skrydstrup grave, but seemingly also around the one in the Borum Eshøj grave (the uncertainty stems from the fact that the latter interment was not professionally excavated).

In Borum Eshøj, the wrap is 110-130x330 cm wide (4.4-3.6

m^2); in Skrydstrup (incidentally, a much taller woman) it is 116x390 cm (4.5 m^2) (Tables 6; 8; 10). Notably, in both graves, the short sides of the wrap were tacked crudely together. The crude tacking is very strange. It argues strongly against identifying the garment as a 'skirt'. Rather, the tacking should be perceived as a symbolic termination of the previous uses of this large, costly, personal and no doubt very important piece of material and the beginning of its final function as a burial cloth.

Interestingly, though often forgotten, the Egtved grave also contained a very large textile covering the dead women and therefore commonly interpreted as a 'blanket' (currently not exhibited at the National Museum in Copenhagen). This majestic textile is 258/250x192/170 cm (5.0/4.3 m^2) (Fig. 17). Due to its size, it should be considered along with the above-mentioned wraps (cf. Alexandersen, Bennike, Hvass & Stærmose Nielsen 1981).

3.2 Long plain skirts

The riddle of the missing covering for the lower part of the bodies of the women of Skrydstrup and Borum Eshøj finds its solution in the additional garments (traditionally termed 'blankets') found in the Skrydstrup grave. In fact, the riddle is solved just by re-naming these 'blankets' as long plain skirts (Fig. 18) (Tables 5-6; 8; 10). Certainly, for all day-to-day chores, skirts, whether the comfortable string skirts, or the long plain ones, were a practical supplement to the blouse or T-shirt.

In size, the two long plain skirts at Skrydstrup much resemble the simple skirts used by African women today: the second either used as a spare or for carrying a small child on the back (Fig. 19). Such a skirt needs no belt, since the two ends are merely rolled together at the waist and over the belly as one would a large bathing towel today. The first of the Skrydstrup specimens is 125x161 cm (2.0 m^2), the second 106x193/179 (2.0/1.9 m^2). Both covered the dead women – like the wrap in the Egtved grave. The Borum Eshøj grave also seems to have held a long plain skirt, perhaps even two: again traditionally interpreted as a 'blanket'.

In fact, the large wrap covering the Egtved woman, if folded and worn with the fold around the waist, could also function as a long plain skirt (192/170x129/125 cm) (cf. Fig. 20; Table 8). The wraps of Borum Eshøj and Skrydstrup cannot be folded into skirts, they would simply part at the waist. However, all three wraps may each be cut into two long plain skirts, and thus serve both as wraps and as other future garments.

By contrast, the 'blanket' in the male Muldbjerg grave was placed *under* the dressed body, as a bed sheet. This blanket is 211x131 cm (2.8 m^2). Another blanket, a fine white and fringed one from the male Trindhøj grave, was cut in two, the one part placed under the head, the other around the feet. This fine blanket is a piece of cloth relatively modest in size, merely 184x133/109 cm (2.4/2.0 m^2), but still larger than the supposed long plain skirts from Skrydstrup. Interestingly, these male blankets, in particular the one from Trindhøj, clearly fall within the range of sizes of the female long plain skirts (Fig. 21). It would seem that the looms were dictating the width of fabrics, with 130/135 cm being the normal maximum, and 120 cm possibly the standard width (cf. §2.2 above).

The great width of the Egtved wrap (up to 192 cm) is remarkable: perhaps it is an import, although there is nothing deviant in either quality or technique that would speak in favour of a foreign textile. At any rate, the loom in question must have been extraordinarily wide, not least if it was a ground-loom. In fact, the very width of the Egtved wrap points to the existence of an upright loom, and probably a warp-weighted one. The same can be said of the very wide blanket from Trindhøj.

Long plain skirts seem also to be present in two Period III graves with only poorly preserved textiles. The first one is Melhøj, discussed in detail below (cf. Bender Jørgensen, Munksgaard & Stærmose Nielsen 1982). Here the long plain skirt ('blanket') was placed on top of the bronzes in the upper part of the grave, above the dead body. The other grave is

42

Hvilshøj, with the 'blanket' (likely a long skirt) placed on top of the cremated bones and the grave goods, including a hair net of the same type as at Skrydstrup (Lomborg 1963).

Indeed, a fully clothed female figurine of the Late Bronze Age from Grevensvænge, Sjælland (Zealand) seems to render a long plain skirt, and not the 'heavy skirt' of traditional wording (Djupedal & Broholm 1952) (Fig. 22). The figurine also seems to be wearing a T-shirt on the upper part of the body (with a large fibula placed on the breast).

Finally, a fully preserved long plain skirt in twill of 177/183x117/121 cm was found with a ninth-century BC Late Bronze Age female bog body from Borremose in Jylland (Jutland) (cf. above and below; van der Sanden 1996, 195 no. 115 (with further references); Jensen 2002, 389f.; Hald 1980, 20f.) (cf. Tables 5-6; 8).

3.3 Wraps

Several reconstructions of the actual wearing of the wrap have been discussed, the most common recent one being that the garment was worn under the armpits, even though this would have considerably impeded movement (Jensen 1979, 39) (Fig. 14). As indicated, the woollen belts in the graves, worn at the waist, are all too light to keep the garment up as a skirt, and there are no traces of fasteners at the shoulders. Another suggestion, that the wrap was worn almost doubled, folded along the length of the garment and held up only by the belt resting on the hips, is not convincing either, however charming the idea of a Nordic parallel to the long multiple-pleated Greek Bronze Age skirts (Harald Hansen 1978). Contact between the two areas, mostly of an indirect nature, is evidenced by metal artefacts and symbolic evidence. But only a very few individuals from the North can have seen the eastern Mediterranean civilisations with their own eyes.

Wearing a wrap as a double skirt folded over the middle and without a belt is theoretically possible but hardly practical, since, as indicated, it would open at the waist. The only wrap which could be worn as a double skirt is the one from Egtved; folded over the middle, it would easily reach around the slim waist and hips (60 cm and 73 cm respectively) of this small woman (Fig. 17; Table 8). Incidentally, a long narrow piece of this wrap was cut off at the burial, perhaps for use in communication with the dead (African parallels) (Hvass 1981, 33).

Though this is mostly forgotten today, M. Hald had already aired reservations about the long skirt hypothesis taken at face value, that is, the textile not being folded double when worn (Broholm & Hald 1919-35, 325f.). Indeed, it would seem that the only way of wearing such a large piece of woollen cloth without folding it is over the head, or at least the shoulders, in much the same way that the men wore their smaller cloaks (cf. Kristiansen 1974, Fig. 14:a-f, with several interesting suggestions). A procession of women with capes over their heads and long skirts – the former likely wraps – is depicted on stone panel nos 7 & 8 of the Early Bronze Age Kivig (Kivik) grave (Randsborg 1993) (Fig. 26). The wrap, apart from being serviceable as a large outer garment, may also have functioned as a bed sheet-cum-cover (men's cloaks and blankets may have served in similar ways).

A Period III grave from Melhøj in Jylland (Jutland) with highly fragmented textiles is difficult to interpret (Bender Jørgensen, Munksgaard & Stærmose Nielsen 1982). The rich artefact assemblage includes two gold spirals and, in bronze, two fibulae, a necklace, a large tutulus, two bracelets, a dagger with bronze ferrule, and an ankle ring. A fine T-shirt and a belt are clearly present; no remains of a string skirt were found. The other garments include what is likely a wrap, recognised at the feet, as well as what is probably a plain long skirt, which covered the middle and upper part of the body, even the head (it was placed on top of the many bronzes in this area of the grave). The suggestion that the latter garment is a man's cloak is less likely on the grounds that we have no other examples of a significant piece of clothing changing gender. Nevertheless, we cannot exclude an otherwise unknown female cloak or cape, in shape perhaps like the short fur capes of the Early Iron Age

(Hald 1980, 47f.: Huldremose, of the second century BC). The existence of a leather cape is perhaps indicated by North German Period III finds of small bronze tutuli covering the upper body of a woman, but a T-shirt is here more likely (Fig. 30).

Thus, at Melhøj, a long plain skirt is the logical choice of interpretation for the garment in question. A number of holes in the cloth may stem from fibulae, one of which was found by the skull (the other was in the stomach region). Also, the long plain skirts at Skrydstrup occupied the same position in the grave as the textile at Melhøj, here interpreted as a skirt. Finally, at Skrydstrup, the lower body was covered by a wrap, which is exactly the garment recognised at the feet of the Melhøj woman.

Particular attention should be paid to the female Borremose bog body, which was once dated to the Iron Age but is in fact of the Late Bronze Age, perhaps as early as the ninth century BC (new C-14 date) (van der Sanden 1996, 195 no. 115 (with further references); Jensen 2002, 389f.). This woman of 20-35 years of age has hair of medium length and was dressed in a long plain skirt of twill weave with fringes (white wool), likely indicating the introduction of an improved type of loom (Bender Jørgensen 1992, 120). The skirt is of the same size as the long plain skirts in the Skrydstrup grave (Hald 1980) (Tables 5-6; 8; Fig. 20). There was even an arrangement for fastening the Borremose skirt, probably with a leather thong.

Thus the Borremose woman confirms a number of the observations and interpretations presented here. This find also represents one of the earliest examples of a new patterned fabric, twill, thought to have been known as early as the thirteenth century BC in Central Europe (Bender Jørgensen 1992, 120). Twill is a common fabric in the Iron Age.

3.4 Male garments

Male garments have received less attention than female ones. Still, they come from the same kind of cloth woven on the same looms. They also display the same careful and economic craftsmanship when cutting and sewing the items.

As a result of the identical width of the wrap from Borum Eshøj and the oval cloaks in the contemporary male graves from the same mound, it has been suggested that the former were turned into men's cloaks upon marriage, women thereafter donning string skirts (Eskildsen & Lomborg 1977; cf. 1976). Support for this idea comes from the identical width of the Skrydstrup wrap and the width of the textile used for producing the larger kidney-shaped cloaks and coats (cf. Fig. 10). However, the suggestion is rather unlikely for a number of reasons, including the old lady of Borum Eshøj being unmarried, and her contemporaries running around in the Nordic winter in string skirts. The observation stands, but is better explained by looms producing cloth of various but standard widths.

At any rate, close analyses of the male garments clearly show that the coats were produced from material left over from making the cloaks (Nielsen 1971; Munksgaard 1974). Even smaller pieces of cloth were employed, as in the case of the female blouses (T-shirts), giving extra length by additions, for functional reasons, often with a different direction of weave (cf. Broholm & Hald 1929-35, 272f. Figs 54-55: Borum Eshøj (old lady); 284f. Figs 67-68: Egtved; Broholm & Hald 1939, 52 Figs 33-34: Skrydstrup). Of course, the fulling (stamping) obliterated traces of many of these manoeuvres.

We have limited knowledge of the amount of textiles available for each adult person – probably modest, to judge from the measures to save cloth, as well as many repairs (cf. Table 10). For women of standing, one may speculate a minimum of one wrap, a couple (or more) of long plain skirts, possibly a string skirt or two, two blouses, plus various minor garments, for instance foot-wraps. For a similar man, a cloak, two coats or loin-cloths, a war-cap and a pixie one (or two), a blanket (to judge from Muldbjerg and Trindhøj), plus various minor garments, including foot-wraps, again as a minimum. A particular problem is the life expectancy of these garments. The demand for wool must have been high, as it was for sheep (which yielded at most only about 1 kg of wool a year). Wool may even have been imported, from the Scandinavian Peninsula for instance.

Not all garments ended up in graves. Furthermore, there would have been items for use as spares and certainly for gifts and special occasions, like the ritual male T-shirt with V-tongues found at Hvidegården, likely a priestly garment (Lomborg 1981) (cf. Fig. 22). Male and even female breech-cloths are an option. Sandals, like the foot-wraps ('socks'), were in use by both genders; seemingly with no significant difference as to shape (Broholm & Hald 1939, 84f.). The sandals are generally very poorly preserved and relatively little is known about them; however, they were tied by a strap which went under the arch of the foot, as seen on shoe-sole images from rock-carvings.

For a whole family and dependants one expects further garments for children, likely made of used adult items, in addition to outer garments of leather and fur for all members of the group. Textiles were probably also used to decorate rooms, for instance on special occasions, as in Classical Antiquity (Wagner-Hasel 2007). The cow-hides of the oak-coffins probably reflect the conditions in bed, where male blankets and female wraps and long plain skirts would have served as additional 'bedclothes', if necessary with the male coat as a supplement. Against the cold, the male pixie cap and female bonnets would have helped. Undressing at night is an option, especially in the summer, but uncertainty reigns. Hygiene was probably at quite a high level among the elite, as indicated by the great care about personal appearance.

All garments from the Bronze Age are without pockets, which call for purses and bags. The men, like the priestly warrior at Hvidegården, carried small leather purses for toiletries and amulets, the women larger net-bags like the one at Borum Eshøj. The blouses of the women have sleeves, while the coats, loincloths and cloaks of the men have no sleeves. Fastening a loincloth or coat poses no problems, but carrying a cloak is only possible with a fastener, likely a leather thong (traces have been found) or a bronze fastener, but only a few graves hold fibulae, buttons and other possible fasteners. The reason could be problems with the use of fibulae or other bronzes directly in the soft standard cloth, where they are hard on the garments. Nevertheless, holes made by fibula pins are observed, as at Melhøj (cf. above).

The elegant cloaks may have been worn in several ways (Fig. 11). To keep an arm free, one could carry it over one shoulder; to keep both arms free one could bundle it for carrying across breast and back, in Scottish fashion, or wind around an arm. In the latter position it would serve as an emergency shield. (Unlike war caps and bronze weapons, shields were not included in the oak-coffin graves.) Carrying the cloak in a balanced fashion over one shoulder gives meaning to the 'collar' in the textile, which is simply to prevent the cloth from bothering neck and ear. Furthermore, the same collar will function as a proper collar when the cloak is carried over both shoulders and kept closed at the front, by a fibula, or by both hands.

3.5 Nakedness

Three groups of finds and monuments allow for discussion of nakedness, or near nakedness, in the Bronze Age, a topic that naturally accompanies a study of clothing. Representations of nakedness are never devoid of cultural meaning. Nakedness may even be a cultural idiom, a style of representation rather than a reference to reality, as in the case of Classical Greece, where the naked body is a way of rendering beauty – youth, strength, health, harmony, etc. Indeed, nakedness signals the unusual, of whatever kind. In the North, Bronze Age rock-carvings are a particular challenge, with almost none of the very many human figures displaying any form of garment.

The first group of Bronze Age finds discussed here comprises human bronze figurines, including anthropomorphic details on artefacts. The second group comprises rare depictions of human beings on bronzes, in particular Late Bronze Age razors (cf. Kaul 1998). The latter might be regarded as 'rock-carvings' on bronzes, but are much better defined as to motifs and dating than are rock-carvings. The third group comprises depictions of human beings in rock-carvings (cf. Burenhult 1983; 1980; Schauer 1985; Malmer 1992; Randsborg 1993; Kaul 1998; 2004; Milstreu & Pøhl 1996; 1999; Coles 2005; etc.) (Tables 11-12).

Figurines. The figurines can be divided into two series. The first series comprises passive naked females; the second series comprises figurines which we know from tenons under the feet to have been part of larger representations. The latter figurines wear some clothing and display various actions.

(1) The figurines of the first series comprise standing naked females, usually with breasts and often vagina emphasised; they display no movement (Fig. 23). Usually they are equipped with necklaces and a belt or another ribbon-like arrangement; the coiffure is not emphasised. They may represent fertility deities like the similar wooden figures from the Early Iron Age of naked women and men, with vagina and phallus emphasised. In fact, a wooden phallic man has recently been dated to the close of the Late Bronze Age (Kaul 2004, 76f. with Figs 9-10). The figure, from Broddenbjerg in Jylland (Jutland), is bearded, a feature unknown in the Bronze Age. The naked female bronze figurines resemble amulets; they are even worn. It has been suggested that they are weights, referring to a common standard of about 100 g and fractiles thereof (Malmer 1992). Notably, they are all from south-eastern regions.

A princely grave from the early Hallstatt Culture (contemporary with the end of the Late Bronze Age in Denmark) at Strettweg in Austria contained a model wagon with a cultic scene centered on an oversized naked standing and belted female figure holding a large bowl on her head and surrounded by much smaller active figures, including mounted warriors, human figures of both sexes, stags, etc. (Egg 1996). The scene looks like a three-dimensional version of a contemporary Nordic rock carving.

(2) The figurines of the second series (with tenons under the feet) are active and partly clothed (Figs 22; 24). The earliest are the two identical male specimens with movable arms and tall

brimmed hats from the Early Bronze Age Period II hoard at
Stokholt (Stockhult) in Skåne (Scania); these are clad in loincloths or the like, the shins are emphasised, likely a way of
rendering youth, strength, and perhaps supernatural physical
activity, for instance long-distance running or jumping high
(Randsborg 1993, 112 Fig. 80). The same feature appears in
early Greek art, in particular of the Geometric period. The
Near Eastern prototypes of such figurines supposedly represent deities (or divine rulers). The hoard also contained several
large cult axes, ordinary axes, a fine neck-collar, fragment of a
large belt-plate, various tutuli, etc.

From Skåne comes a Late Bronze Age hoard with two
masked male heads decorating a piece of horse gear (Larsson
1973-74; cf. Randsborg 1993, 104 Fig. 76 below). The masks
carry a bird's beak (on the prow), horns, and the outline of a
cult axe (on the crown); in use of symbols, the masks resemble
the famous bossed Viksø helmets from Sjælland (Zealand),
which also have horns, a beak, and a double image of a web-
footed bird, in addition to tube attachments for a horse mane or
tail, feathers, and the like (Norling-Christensen 1943). The
knob on a staff (sceptre?) from Glasbakke (Glasbacka) in Hal-
land displays a masked human face with a beak on the prow;
there are two different eyes: one shining, one 'dull', perhaps
representing day and night (Randsborg 1993, 104 Fig. 76 top).
The profile of the knob resembles the head of the cowled figures, probably women, seen in processions on the rock-carved
slabs of the famous Kivig (Kivik) grave (of about 1300 BC), from
Skåne (Scania) (Randsborg 1993). The different eyes even re-
call the one blind eye of the Nordic supreme god, Odin.

Sjælland (Zealand) provides a Late Bronze Age hoard from
Grevensvænge with twin male figurines wearing horned helmets (Engelhardt 1871, 452f.) (Djupedal & Broholm 1952) (Fig.
22). The hoard consists of the two helmeted figurines seated on
their heels, or dancing: similar poses on rock-carvings display
figures with only half bent knees or less (Coles 2005, 19f. Figs
18; 21; 23; 27; 49; 161; 172; 175; 187; 196; etc.). The two figures
are holding a large cult axe in their right and left hand respec-

tively; the other hand is on the breast, fingers outstretched, thumb up: likely a religiously loaded gesture of respect. As mentioned above, the two men are dressed in belted T-shirts open at the sides and ending in a V, serving as a breechcloth; strangely, the men are also wearing necklaces, adding to the gender confusion (it is hardly a matter of the neck of the T-shirt). The large size of cult axes may stem from the fact that they belong to (or are consecrated to) the gods. The particular gesture is also seen on early Greek so-called Daedalic sculpture of the seventh century BC, as well as other sculpture. It may represent a greeting, perhaps expressing deference.

The fact that the large cult axes are held by men of ordinary size (the size of cult axes is known from actual finds) may indicate that the figures should be regarded as ordinary human beings dressed up for cultic events.

The Grevensvænge deposit also holds the figurine of a fully dressed woman seemingly wearing a blouse or T-shirt (a double-disc fibula is on the breast), and a belted long plain skirt. (Since this figurine is known only from old drawings, the 'double disc fibula' may be the woman's breasts. However, the connecting line (the 'bow' of the fibula) and the very high position of the 'breasts' argue against it.) Originally, this figurine, which is also wearing a necklace, had a partner. Finally, the find holds three identical women in acrobatic pose, wearing only a short string skirt (the breasts are marked); the acrobats have fine coiffures and each wears a necklace.

From Fårdal, northern Jylland (Jutland), comes a rich Late Bronze Age hoard of Period V with a 'seated' (dancing) woman in only a short string skirt, necklace and bracelet; the coiffure is a long pony tail (Broholm 1943-49/Vol. III M 199) (Fig. 24). The eyes are very big and gilded, as if illuminated from within. The right hand (with a bracelet) is holding a string (of organic material), likely the leash for a snake also belonging to the representation. There is even a collection of stag heads, or horse heads, perhaps masked, with mounted horns; a twin stag head has at the centre a web-footed bird. Otherwise, the hoard contained heavy female parade accessories (two hanging vessels and large tutulus, a necklace, various bracelets, etc., plus a prestigious metal-studded belt).

The female with gilded eyes is likely a deity, or the companion of a deity; the holy sun is living inside her, shining out through her eyes. The snake appears on the images of razors as an assistant animal in the daily journeys of the sun (Kaul 2004, 241f., including Figs 66-67).

From a hoard of Late Bronze Age Period V at Fangel Torp, Fyn (Funen) comes a 'kneeling' (dancing) woman with both hands on her breasts. The item must have served as knob on a staff or sceptre (Thrane 1983). This woman seems to be completely naked apart from a belt, a necklace and earrings, plus, seemingly, a large tutulus on the lower back.

To these figurines should be added a number of Late Bronze Age representations, mostly of females, as part of various artefacts, including a standing women (handle on knife) from Itzehoe in Holsten (Holstein) dated to Late Bronze Age Period V (Broholm & Hald 1929-35, 121 Fig. 115). The woman is dressed in only a short string skirt (breast visible) and is holding a vessel; she seems to be belted, as well as equipped with sandals. The coiffure is fine; earrings, necklaces and spiral arm-rings complete the appearance.

Other knives display only heads and upper bodies, including a Late Bronze Age Period V specimen from Javngyde, Central Jylland (Jutland) with a finely coiffured female head with ear-rings and a necklace (Schauer 1985, 189 Abb. 66:3). The head on a Period V knife from Holsten (Holstein) also seems to represent a woman (necklace) (Schauer 1985, 189 Abb. 66:4). From Simris, Skåne comes a Period V knife-handle with the upper body of a naked human being of unknown gender (male?); in a particular gesture, the one hand is on the breast, as in the Grevensvænge find, the fingers are outstretched and the thumb is up (Althin 1945, 77f. Abb. 32; Schauer 1985, Tafel 16:3). A pin from Horne, Fyn (Funen) carries the head of a coiffured woman with earrings and necklace (Schauer 1985, 189 Abb. 66:2). Finally, a female head that once had earrings, though they are missing today, constitutes the handle of a razor from Early Bronze Age Period II, found in a rich male grave from Gerdrup, Sjælland (Zealand) (AK I, Find 473).

Humans depicted on bronzes. Human beings depicted on bronzes comprise the following. From Vognsild, northern Jylland (Jutland) comes a symbolically highly important razor of Late Bronze Age Period IV with two probably male figures running (or rather dancing) onboard a ship (Fig. 25). The figures appear very large compared to the ship, they are horned and carry a cult axe in one hand; shins are emphasised and seemingly wrapped; there is no other indication of clothing (Kaul 1998, no. 210). No strokes indicating the crew can be seen. To the back of the ship stands a huge, likely naked, female figure (ponytail), perhaps belted, the shins are emphasised and seemingly wrapped. The woman is holding a leash for a snake (cf. the above figurine from Fårdal, also from northern Jylland). All the human figures are more than mere matchstick shapes.

From Tvilum, Central Jylland (Jutland) comes a Late Bronze Age Period V razor with a ship carrying two very large (compared to the ship) figures with raised hands, rays are emanating from their heads and there is no indication of clothing; ordinary crew paddlers (or perhaps other rays) are marked as small strokes along the railing (Kaul 1998, no. 273). Again we have fully outlined bodies. From 'Slesvig', southern Jylland (Jutland) comes a razor with two seated human figures (no indication of clothing) paddling a ship. The figures are very large indeed in relation to the ship and may represent deities, as likely explained by the rays emanating from their heads; ordinary crew strokes are perhaps placed along the keel, but these strokes are probably also rays (Kaul 1998, no. 366). In spite of the fact that the figures are made with various bundles of lines, the bodies seem full.

From the Bremen area, northwest Germany, comes a well known Late Bronze Age Period V razor with a single huge person, again with rays emanating from the head; other rays seem to come from the boat itself; the figure is drawn in bundles of lines, but is still rather full; the knees are bent as if seated or dancing (cf. the figurines from Grevensvænge and Fårdal above, etc.); there is no indication of clothing (Sprock-hoff 1954, 94 Abb. 30:3; Kaul 1998/Vol. I, 250 Fig.196). The figure is holding an item in one hand, which normally is taken to be a paddle oar. However, this 'oar' is very broad and in the shape of an '8'; perhaps it is a stringed instrument. In front of the human figure is a strange, perhaps hybrid beaked figure: a bird-snake?

A couple of razors carry strangely distorted human shapes placed onboard ships in hallucination-like patterns, thus a Late Bronze Age Period V specimen from Flemløse, Fyn (Funen) where emphasised 'dancing' shins, thighs and bodies can be dimly seen (Kaul 1998, no. 105). Another such razor, also of Period V, comes from Borgdorf in Slesvig; thighs are emphasised, heads are beak-like (Kaul & Freudenberg 2007, 98f.). Finally, a tutulus from Late Bronze Age Period V carries outlines of dancing men (?) and, possibly, horse heads; these images may thus repre-sent the sun god and his mount in perpetual movement; no clothing is depicted (Kaul 2004, 343f. with Fig. 164).

In conclusion, it would seem that the figurines and human beings on bronzes all represent deities and their companions, or, at the very least, initiated members of cult groups. Some figurines (with tenons) are parts of larger representations of 'stories', in fact, Nordic Bronze Age myths. Others (the stand-ing naked females) carry a meaning in their own right; possibly they were amulets, likely representing a fertility goddess. Such interpretation is supported by representations of divine beings (and companions) on a few razors and other bronzes. Naked-ness is a typical feature, even though the abdomen is covered on the figurines representing myths. Thus, nakedness is linked with the supernatural and its manifestations; possibly, naked-ness was also a feature in the cult, or at least a way of rendering religious significance. Incidentally, nakedness would prohibit mid-winter outdoor performances; the short string skirts also point to the summer as the period of cult festivals.

Humans depicted in rock-carvings. This takes us to the human beings on rock-carvings, always depicted as if seen from far away (Table 12) (Fig. 27). The limits of images on the rock-carvings are usually difficult to define, and the representations often difficult to date. Some rock-carvings are mere symbols, like the wheel-cross (outline of a chariot-wheel), probably standing for astronomical movement. Looking at the human beings, we detect very little information on dress; the 'match-stick' people on the rock-carvings (nearly) all seem to be naked. Male sex is evident in quite a number of phalloi – again emphasising nakedness (and stressing fecundity), but most humans have no indication of their sex. Female breasts are never seen and female genitalia almost never marked, but the many non-phallic human figures may be females. Nakedness is evidently a cultural phenomenon but may also have been a symbol of otherworldly phenomena.

Accessories, including the ones already known from the figurines, are common on the rock-carvings. Movement comprises processions, also on board ships, dancing, playing on lur horns, brandishing large cult axes, weapons (even fighting) and shields, the latter likely of the thin cult variety with calendar information in the decoration (cf. Randsborg & Christensen 2006, 59ff.); furthermore, carrying and display of models and other special items, including sun-images – a clear indication of cult scenes, various plays, and, of course, very much traffic with ships. The ship even takes on symbolic meaning as a carrier of the sun across the skies and through the night, thus assisting the horse of the Early Bronze Age Sun Chariot from Trundholm, Sjælland (Zealand) and similar images and ideas (Kaul 2004, 251 Fig. 87).

At Kivig (Kivik) in Skåne (Scania), a huge cairn covers the famous grave cist with formal framed rock-carving panels on the eight slabs of the long sides (Randsborg 1993) (Fig. 26). The images comprise a display of religious and status symbols, including a tall brimmed hat, large cult axes and a model boat. Furniture is lacking, however, even the princely folding stools. The motifs also comprise religious symbols such as wheel crosses and mushroom figures (likely symbols of the night); nearby horses are probably for pulling the sun. Manned boats are also depicted, as well a series of highly interesting scenes, including driving a chariot, parading warriors, blowing of lur horns, a likely duel, wild animals, and rows of cowled figures, probably women, in wraps arranged with a beak over the head like the knob of the staff from Glasbakke (Glasbacka) discussed above. The Kivig (Kivik) grave displays the full array of symbols, artefacts and scenes with human beings and animals seen in the carvings on natural rocks. The only thing lacking at Kivig (Kivik) is men with phalloi, so common elsewhere on rock-carvings. Even at Kivig (Kivik), the only clothing seen is the wraps of the cowled figures.

It might be that rock carvings with human beings, concentrated in certain geographical regions, like Bohuslen, or south-eastern Skåne (Scania), and even Bornholm, are testimonies to cultic meetings and feasts, where myths have been turned into plays, the many ships being both means of transportation and platforms for competing performances. Such occasions would also have served very many other ends: political negotiation, marriage arrangements, social and economically motivated exchanges, etc. Other travel would have been to the homes of kings and magnates, likely of the type famously undertaken by the Queen of Sheba to King Solomon of Israel (1 Kings 10:1-13) (see §5.2 below).

Being naked, or almost naked – the opposite of dressed – is in the Bronze Age linked with deities, their companions and initiated followers. It may well have been a significant element in cult performances, reminiscent of West African respect shown traditionally towards high-ranking persons, and towards spirits and deities at sacred localities, by baring the upper part of the body.

Figures

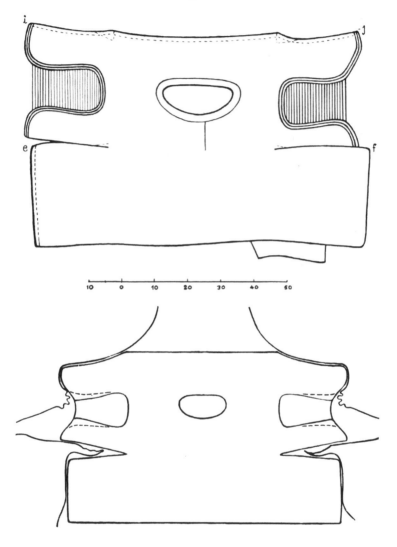

Fig. 1. Pattern of the embroidered Skrydstrup blouse, and the same superimposed on the half-skin of a roe stag. After Broholm & Hald 1939; Hald 1980.

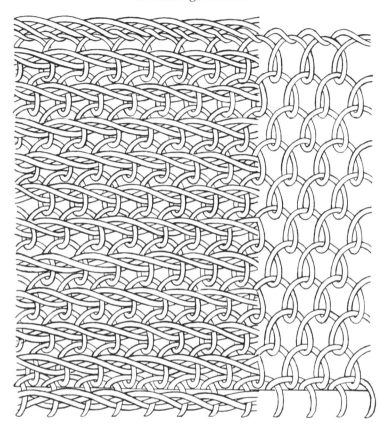

Fig. 2. Diagram of the embroidery on the neck of the blouse of the Skrydstrup woman, Denmark. After Broholm & Hald 1939.

Figures

Fig. 3. (a) Blouse (T-shirt) and (b) string skirt from the Egtved grave. The strings of the skirt are united at both top and bottom; wound twice around the lower body, such a skirt is much less transparent than often supposed. After Broholm & Hald 1929-35. (c) 2.5 m long woollen string with animal hair straws, found in a small box in the Egtved grave. Likely part of a sanitary napkin with fasteners, to which belong mosses and a wad of lambs' wool, and, of course, a piece of cloth or napkin. After Lomborg 1963.

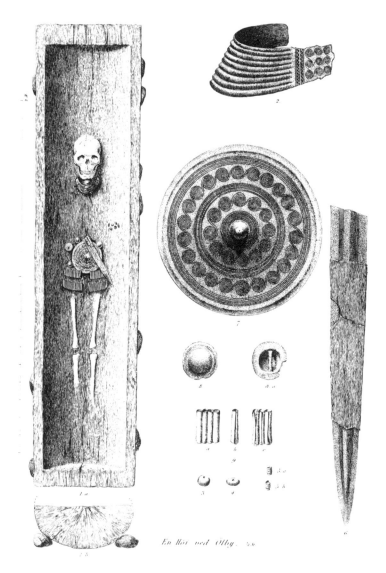

Fig. 4. Bronze tubes used for decorating a lost string skirt, and other bronzes, found in an Early Bronze Age Period II grave at Ølby, Sjælland (Zealand). After Boye 1896.

Figures

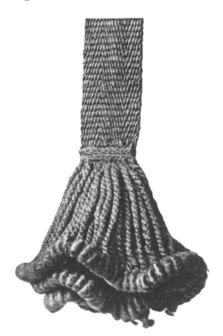

Fig. 5. Tassel and part of the elegant long decorative belt from Borum Eshøj (old woman). Note the elegant patterning produced by threads spun in alternate directions. After Broholm & Hald 1929-35.

Fig. 6. Thick war cap from the male Muldbjerg grave, Jylland (Jutland). Note the exquisite workmanship. After Broholm & Hald 1929-35.

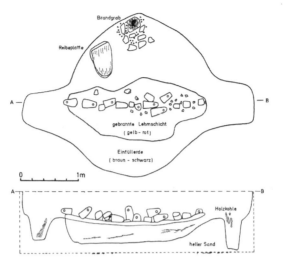

Fig. 7. Remains of a Late Bronze Age warp-weighted loom from a settlement at Wallwitz at Burg in northern Central Germany. A cremation grave of Period IV is placed in the weaving pit. After Stahlofen 1978.

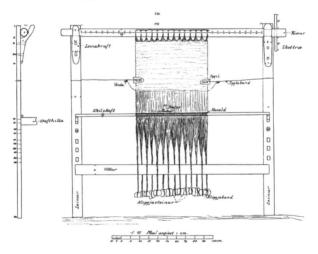

Fig. 8. Simple upright warp-weighted loom from Færøerne (the Faeroe Islands), *c.* 1700 AD. Museum of Thorshavn. After Broholm & Hald 1929-35. Note that the loom-weights are stones. A loom from the Roman Iron Age in Denmark measures 180 cm between the two uprights, nearly the same as the Faeroe Island loom (Broholm & Hald 1929-35, 300, note 3; Hald 1980, 199 Fig. 236a).

Figures

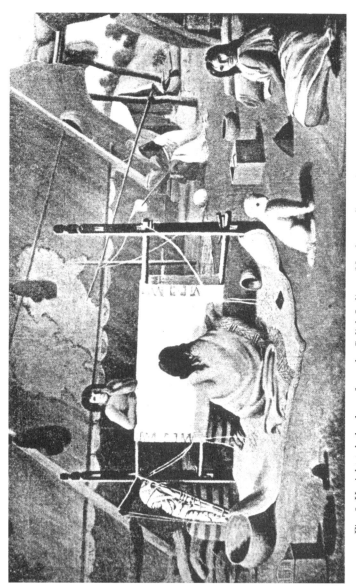

Fig. 9. Upright tubular loom from the Salish Indians (Northwest Coast of America, border areas between USA and Canada). Painting of the mid-nineteenth century. After Birket-Smith 1937.

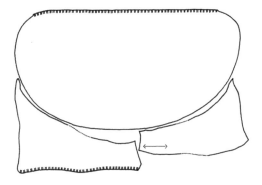

Fig. 10. Making of a
male kidney-shaped
cloak and coat from a
certain width and
length of textile: the
cases of Muldbjerg
and Trindhøj, both
Jylland (Jutland).
After Munksgaard
1974; cf. Nielsen 1971.

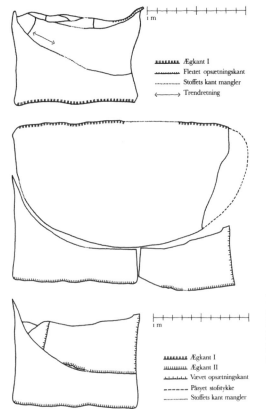

Ægkant I
Flettet opsætningskant
Stoffets kant mangler
Trendretning

Ægkant I
Ægkant II
Vævet opsætningskant
Påsyet stofstykke
Stoffets kant mangler

Fig. 11. Reconstru-
ction of male Early
Bronze Age dress,
Muldbjerg style. After
Munksgaard 1974
(drawing K. Malling).

64

Figures

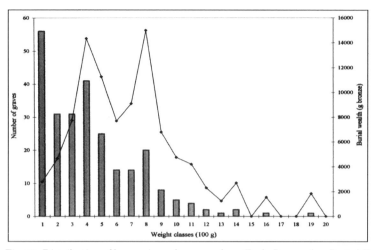

Fig. 12. Distribution of bronze in male graves from Early Bronze Age Period II in Denmark (histograms). Unbroken line = amount of bronze in each grave class. After Randsborg & Christensen 2006.

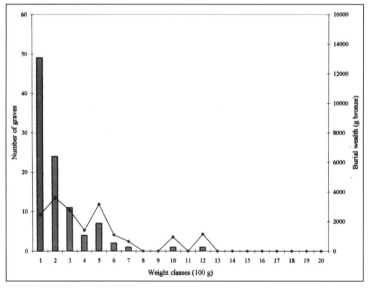

Fig. 13. Distribution of bronze in female graves from Early Bronze Age Period II in Denmark (histograms). Unbroken line = amount of bronze in each grave class. After Randsborg & Christensen 2006.

Fig. 14. Traditional suggestion – one of many – for the mode of wearing a thick 'heavy skirt' in Skrydstrup and Borum Eshøj style: a 'wrap' in present terminology. After Jensen 1979 (drawing F. Bau). I suggest that such reconstructions are all wrong, and that the 'blankets' found in the same graves were in fact worn as long plain skirts, the wraps merely as outer garments (or used for other purposes).

Fig. 15. Large wrap, shrouding the lower part of the body of the Borum Eshøj women when buried (double); note the poor joining of the short sides: *c.* 4 m^2. After Broholm & Hald 1929-35.

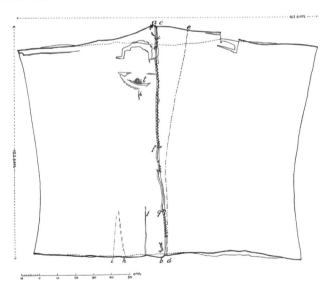

Figures

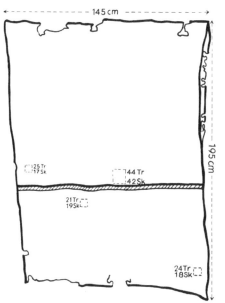

Fig. 16. Large wrap, shrouding the lower part of the body of the Skrydstrup women when buried (double); note the poor joining of the short sides: 4.5 m^2. After Broholm & Hald 1939.

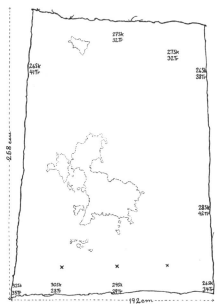

Fig. 17. Large wrap, traditionally termed 'blanket', from the Egtved grave: 4.5-5 m^2. After Broholm & Hald 1929-35.

67

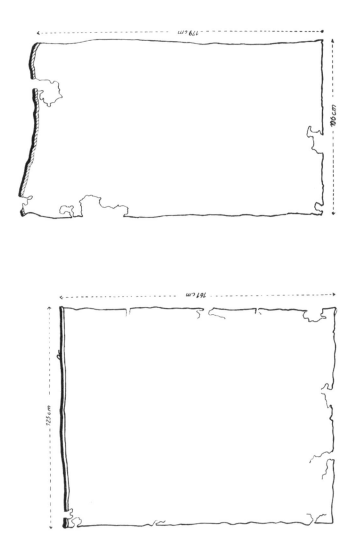

Fig. 18. Two long plain skirts, traditionally termed 'blankets', from the Skrydstrup grave: 2.0 & 2.0/1.9 m². After Broholm & Hald 1939.

Fig. 19. Contemporary West African saleswomen and customers at the new market of Bohicon town in southern Bénin. Common use of T- and other shirts is noted, as well as a variety of applications for a piece of cloth the size of the long plain skirts in the Skrydstrup grave (cf. Figs 18 & 20), including long plain shirt, extra skirt, headdress, or sling for carrying a baby on the back. Modernised full dresses can also be seen. Photo: Author.

Bronze Age Textiles

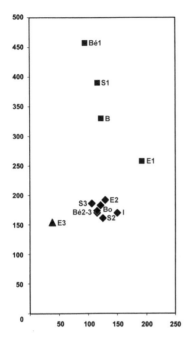 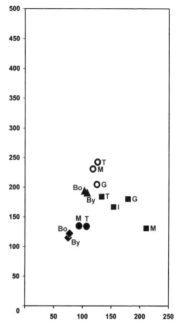

Fig. 20. Correlation of lengths and widths of selected larger female Bronze Age and other garments (skirts, wraps, etc.); cf. Table 8.

Diamond = long plain skirt. Triangle = string skirt. Square = wrap. (Note that long wraps may be cut into two long plain skirts.) B = Borum Eshøj wrap (old woman). E1 = Egtved wrap; E2 = Egtved wrap folded and worn as a double long plain skirt; E3 = Egtved string skirt. S1 = Skrydstrup wrap; S2 = first Skrydstrup long plain skirt; S3 = second Skrydstrup long plain skirt. Bo = Borremose long plain skirt. I = Islay, Scottish traditional plaid (also coat). Bé1 = Bénin traditional burial wrap; Bé2-3 = Bénin, recent long plain skirts for women and/or for carrying a baby (identical in size).

Fig. 21. Correlation of lengths and widths of selected larger pieces of male Bronze Age and other garments (cloaks, coats, loincloths, and blankets); cf. Table 7. Circle = cloak (kidney-shaped). Triangle = cloak (oval). Dot = coat. Diamond = loincloth. Square = blanket (/wrap). Bo = Borum Eshøj, old man. By = Borum Eshøj, young man. G = Guldhøj. M = Muldbjerg. T = Trindhøj. I = Islay; Scottish traditional coat (also plaid). G = Ghana kente cloth (blanket, or wrap).

70

Figures

Fig. 22. Late Bronze Age figurines from Grevensvænge near Næstved, Sjælland (Zealand): drawing from the late eighteenth century. After Djupedal & Broholm 1952; cf. Lomborg 1981.The small figures belong to a larger model representation: To the left, two men sitting in priestly V-shaped T-shirts wearing horned helmets and carrying over-sized cult-axes; a belt is visible. Above, a dancing naked woman in only a very short string skirt (one of three identical figurines); a necklace is visible. To the right, a standing woman in T-shirt and long plain skirt; necklace, belt, and a double-disc fibula (on the breast) are visible (cf. Fig. 20). Only one horned man and one dancer have survived to the present day; they confirm the relative accuracy of the drawings.

71

Fig. 23. Naked female figurine from Farø,
Sjælland (Zealand). After Müller 1921.

Figures

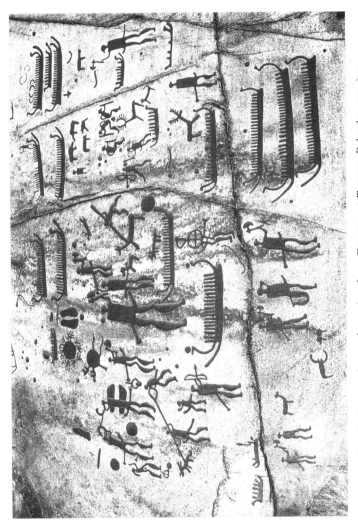

Fig. 27. Bronze Age rock-carving from Fossum at Tanum, Bohuslen province, Swedish-Norwegian borderlands on the Kattegat (Cattegat). After Coles 2005.

75

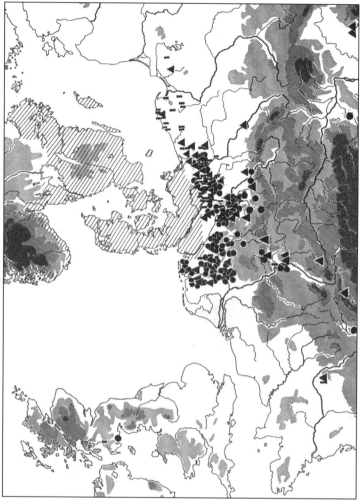

Fig. 29. Distribution of Nordic bronzes from Late Bronze Age Periods IV-V outside the Nordic cultural area. After Thrane 1975a. Vertical dash = sword; triangle = women's artefact; circle = other items. The many Nordic items near the core area reflect general interaction, including high ranking marriages; the more distant ones rare royal meetings and individual contact, the latter possibly through several links, and collection of scrap metal.

Fig. 30. Reconstruction of a dressed Early Bronze Age bog-body from Emmer-Erfscheienveen, the Netherlands (Holland): *c.* 1300 or thirteenth century BC. The person is primarily dressed in hide and fur of sheep (cap), calf (cloak), and deer (shoes), but wore a woollen coat. After van der Sanden 1996. Details of the coat are guesswork.

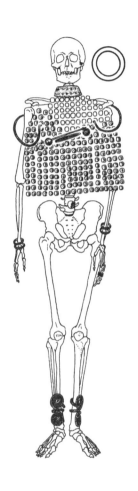 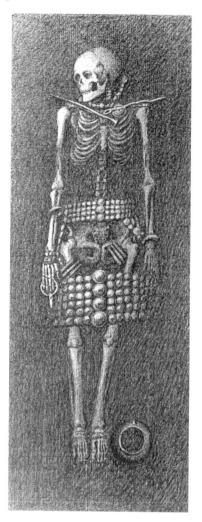

Fig. 31. Female grave of Early Bronze Age Period III from Lübz, Mecklenburg, North Germany. After Sprockhoff 1939. The many light bronze tutuli belong to a T-shirt, or perhaps a cape.

Fig. 32. Female Middle Bronze Age grave from Hügel 5 (Hügelgruppe XIV), Mühlthal at Starnberg (near München), Oberbayern, South Germany. After Naue 1894. The many added-on small tutuli seem to indicate a short string skirt; the long dress pins likely a wrap of some kind.

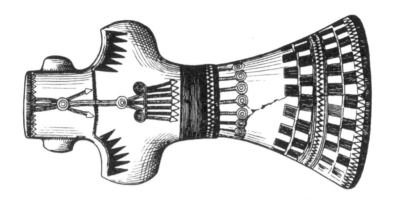

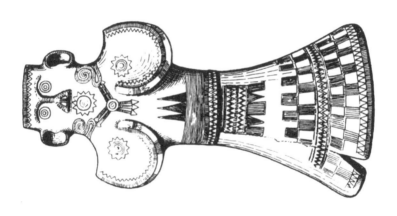

Fig. 33. Female figurine from Kliċevac near Smederevo, Serbia. 34 cm tall; it disappeared during World War I; local Middle Bronze Age, around 1400 BC. After Müller-Karpe 1980.

4

Cultural Aspects

4.1 Seasons

It has been suggested that the rather short string skirt, apart from being used in cult by junior members of performer groups (cf. Fig. 22), is a summer garment. Testing this proposition, the period of burial is established on the basis of plants included in the oak-coffins, and – secondarily – on the basis of the orientation of the coffin (cf. Randsborg & Nybo 1984). In most regions, the supine dead person 'faces' east and sunrise at the time of burial, the head being in the western end of the coffin. However, on eastern Sjælland (Zealand), and further east, in the Skåne (Scania) Countries, including Bornholm, the dead person usually faces west and sunset at the time of burial. Thus, the same phenomenon is expressed in two different ways, suggesting both a unity of culture and 'ethnic' distinctions.

The idea of the string skirt as a summer garment is basically true, as transpires from Table 6 (cf. Table 13), where female graves, most with string skirts (often demonstrated by series of bronze sheet metal tubes), clearly cluster in the warmer period April to September, even though there are no certain burials from the warmest period, May to July (only the very beginning of May is an option). The women of Egtved and Skrydstrup seem to have been buried in the same period (September), in spite of their different skirts. The possible long skirt of the Melhøj grave belongs to a burial of the summer half of the year (early May or early August). The higher number of women than men in the tables is due to the relative ease of identifying metal-decorated string skirts. Overrepresentation of the string skirt is a factor to be taken into account. At any rate, there is

80

support for the hypothesis that the string skirt was mainly a summer garment, and not only a cultic dress, at least not in the Early Bronze Age.

However few the observations, it is clear from Table 7 (cf. Table 13) that most of the men with preserved textiles whose burials can be seasonally determined were buried during the colder months, October to March. This is in accordance with the thick war- and other caps, the cloaks, and the blankets in the coffins (cf. Randsborg & Nybo 1984, 175). Again, there are no burials during the warmest period May to July. Unless burial was undertaken only in certain periods, the cold months must have been particularly stressful to the men (to everybody, one would expect); women would have suffered from the complications of childbirth, a great killer in pre-modern societies, all year round.

Looking at the numerous common graves with no textiles preserved, only bronzes etc., the seasonal trends are the same. The peculiar male emphasis on the sunrise period around 95°, in fact, *c.* 80° to 110° East, i.e. mid-March or the start of October (or mid-February to the end of March, or mid-September to mid-October, to be more precise), is evident (Randsborg & Nybo 1984, 168 Fig. 14). Two phases are given, since the sun rises at a particular point in both the first half of the year and the second half.

We may have identified the main periods of warfare (and male casualties). If so, it is probably the latter period (autumn) rather than the former one, considering the demands of agriculture and ranching in the earlier part of the year; however, both are possible.

4.2 Sanitation

Menstruation and other issues of sanitation and hygiene are almost unknown areas as far as much of Antiquity is concerned; for Prehistory, guesswork reigns. Egypt provides a few glimpses from the Bronze Age in the rich Deir-el Medina documents, invaluable testimonies to daily life (Toivari-Viitala

2001, 162f., with further references; cf. McDowell 2002, including 59f., the quotation given below). Deir-el Medina is a royal craftman's village near Thebes.

> Year 1, third month of winter, day 15. This day, given clothes to the washermen.
> What came from/via him in the third month of winter, day 16.
> Given to them at the riverbank to launder:
> kilts 10
> loincloths 8
> sanitary towels 5
>
>   Ancient Egyptian laundry list from
>   Deir-el Medina, *c*. 1300-1100 BC

In a small birch-bark box in the Egtved grave, standing next to the head, a strange nearly 2.5 m long woollen string was found, with six knots, a possible loop, and a 8-9 cm long stretch of knots and windings (Thomsen 1929-35; Lomborg 1963, 42f.; 1964; Alexandersen, Bennike, Hvass & Stærmose Nielsen 1981, 35; cf. Hvass 1981; Jensen 1998, 18) (Fig. 3c; cf. Table 9). Two knots at the ends of the string are wound around tufts of cattle-tail hair. In the middle, several knotted tufts of cattle-tail hair are held to the string by a winding of thinner string. Some of the knots of the string may be explained by multiple uses, others by tying together shorter strings (revealed by different numbers of threads). The individual stretches between the knots are 44, 33, 97, 18 and 53 cm, respectively, making it impossible that the string was used for measuring (Lomborg 1963, 46 note 21; calibrated lengths after shrinking). Most knots, windings and tufts of cattle-tail hair are at the middle of the longest stretch. The animal hair is puzzling. Interpretation of the string as a protective 'amulet' belt is possible, but it was not wound around the dead body.

It has been suggested that the string represents the remains of a hair net of cattle-tail hair with a long woollen string for tying it around the head (model Skrydstrup). The claim that the strings of cattle-tail are inter-woven is less likely. More decisively, a woollen string (with a few human hairs), 1.3 m long, was found at the back of the head of the young Egtved woman; this woollen string was meant to keep her hair together at the neck. Also, the hair of the Egtved woman is rather short, which argues against the use of a hairnet of the type found in the Borum Eshøj grave (of wool), or of the type found in the Skrydstrup grave. The Skrydstrup woman wore her hair very long indeed and finely arranged in a full and tall coiffure covered by a net (notably, of long horse-tail hair), and, potentially, a bonnet, which was also included in the grave. Incidentally, a hair net of animal hair (horse-tail?) was found in the Hvilshøj grave, likely of Period III (Lomborg 1963).

An alternative idea is to interpret the knotted string in the small box at Egtved as part of a sanitary arrangement or belt, for which a piece of fur or cloth is also needed. The knotted middle part may be explained by a need to thicken the string on the vagina. An appropriately sized piece of cloth is not present in the small box, which, however, held sweet-smelling heather (mainly leaves), absorbent mosses, and a wad of fine lambs' wool. The brush-like tufts of thick cattle-tail hair at the middle of the string would have been helpful in securing the materials in place. Seemingly the only candidate for a piece of cloth in the Egtved grave is the textile used to wrap the cremated bones of a 5/6-year-old child. This cloth is a maximum 27x110 cm, and could actually serve the purpose if folded to a size of 0.1 m² (cf. below and §4.2) (Table 9). Based on excavation sketches and photos, remains of cloth may have been found on the legs (especially the knees) of the Egtved woman (Alexandersen, Bennike, Hvass & Stærmose Nielsen 1981, 35f. Fig. 8). This observation, if correct, is omitted in the excavation report and publication, as well as in discussions of the dress (Thomsen 1929-35; Broholm & Hald 1929-35; 1940). Perhaps it is only a matter of imprints and/or fragments of the wrap.

Similar sanitary arrangements are known from the recent past in Europe (as across the world), including crocheted pads (Denmark, etc.). Materials for absorbing menstrual blood include mosses (Lithuania), rabbit skin and cotton-grass (Greenland Inuit), sheepskin (USA), and absorbing pieces of cloth, 'towels' or 'napkins' (various historical and ethnographic sources, often difficult to find, including www.mum.org).

The girth of the hips of the Egtved women is a modest *c.* 73 cm, the waist only about 60 cm, as measured, respectively, by the string skirt resting on the hips (the band being 3 cm above the pubic hair), and the 1.75 m long tasselled ornamental belt tied around the waist (Thomsen 1929-35, 187f.). The height of the Egtved woman is 1.59-1.60 m; the upper part of the pubic hair is 0.77 m from the crown of the head, the lower part 0.86 m; thus, the hips are 0.74 m from the crown. To judge from excavation photos, the distance between the belt and the upper edge of the string skirt is about 11 cm, or a little more. The crotch is thus about 23 cm below the waist (the actual stretch from waist to crotch – front or back – is a little more), which again seems a very modest distance. From these measures, one may surmise that the small Egtved woman is actually younger than the 'about 17 years of age' given her by anthropologists, perhaps even of the age of her first menstruation. The length of the string (2.45 m) would have permitted it to be tied once around the waist and to run between the legs three times, giving ample extra length for tying knots. A longer hip string (with shorter crotch ones) is unlikely: worn on the hips, such an arrangement would tend to slip at the crotch.

It is possible that further sanitary arrangements are present in Early Bronze Age graves. In addition to the major garments, the Skrydstrup grave held a folded, rather small square piece of cloth of only a little more than 0.1 m^2 – a towel perhaps (Table 9; cf. cover illustration). It was placed near the jaw. A sanitary napkin is an option but the Skrydstrup grave holds no string for fastening. Nonetheless, the simple 2.15 m long belt from the grave – notably with no tassels – wound around the wrap, covering the lower part of the body, may have served exactly this purpose. A baby's napkin is unlikely, due to the woman's young age and supposedly unmarried status (if babies' napkins were used at all in the Bronze Age). However, a symbolic reference to a status not reached at death cannot be dismissed, as in the cases of Egtved (child and mother) and Borum Eshøj, the young man (sword and full commander) (cf. §4.4). In the Skrydstrup grave, the 'towel' even occupies the same position at the head as the small box at Egtved, containing the string and materials for a sanitary belt. The size of the Skrydstrup cloth, when folded, complies with historically known sanitary napkins (cf. Table 9).

At Borum Eshøj, the old woman's grave, unfortunately unprofessionally excavated, may also hold a sanitary napkin, heavily stamped and in the form of a thick rectangular 'towel', 48x27 cm (a little more than 0.1 m^2) (Table 9). A pectoral cloth has been suggested – in late nineteenth-century style (Boye 1896, 61). But a breechcloth for the elderly lady comes to mind, likely held up by the second simpler belt of the find, 2.06 m long and less than 2 cm wide. The fine belt with tassels from the same grave is supposedly decorative, as in the case of Egtved (cf. Fig. 5). The Borum Eshøj towel may thus have served an intimate purpose for a woman of progressive age. In fact, a sanitary napkin may be used as a breechcloth, and vice versa.

There are no napkins in male graves, but a possible male breechcloth of 97x9.5 cm (0.1 m^2) has been found in a Period III grave at Nybøl in Jylland (Jutland) (Boye 1896, 107f.; Pl. XXII:A1) (Tables 7; 9). It is quite narrow, like the suggested female sanitary arrangements. The idea that it is a belt is likely wrong, since both male and female belts are narrow, much longer and made in a different technique (tablet weaving). If not a breechcloth, a scarf is an option (though it is still quite narrow); another option is a rather broad and short puttee, even though only one was found in the grave.

Finally, a fine rather broad fringed 'belt' in openwork comes from a grave in Bredhøj, Måbjerg in Jylland (Jutland) (Boye 1896, 24f., Pl. II:B1-2; AK X, 4815;A) (cf. Table 7). The item is only 105 cm long (or even less) and about 5 cm wide; in other words, the same length as the garment from Nybøl. It was found together with a small dagger. The garment is too narrow and open for a breechcloth, and its ornamental character, in-

cluding the fringes, certainly speaks against a sanitary function. If not a belt, it is perhaps a headband. The fringes
resemble the ones on the male belt in Trindhøj, which, incidentally, is very long, and 3 cm wide (Broholm & Hald 1929-35,
239 with 240 Fig. 26). A contemporary belt with fringes comes
from a likely male grave at Itzehoe in Holsten (Holstein); this
belt is 2.5 cm wide (Schlabow 1938; cf. AK XVIII 9407G). The
decorative belt from Borum Eshøj (old woman) is also 3 cm
wide (Fig. 5); the simple belt at Skrydstrup is 3-4 cm wide.

A piece of cloth may serve several functions – hygienic,
handkerchief, scarf, sock, even puttee, etc. But, as always, the
symbolic implications of the oak-coffin grave goods and their
arrangements should also be borne in mind. Reports on sanitary arrangements go back to the laundry lists of the New
Kingdom of Ancient Egypt (above, p. 82). A telling literary
quote about the female Alexandrian scholar Hypatia (from the
Byzantian Suda encyclopaedia of *c.* 975 AD) relates to the
advances of a lovesick young man, whom Hypatia (killed 415
AD) was trying to scare off with the help of her own soiled
sanitary napkins:

> ... She brought some of her female rags and threw them
> before him, showing him the signs of her unclean origin,
> and said, 'You love this, O youth, and there is nothing
> beautiful about it.'

4.3 Status

For a number of reasons, it seems logical to ascribe married (or
widow) status to the strong old woman of Borum Eshøj, rich in
textiles: long hair, elaborate bonnet-like hair net, blouse (T-
shirt), one or more long plain skirts, wrap, etc., dagger, and
rich jewellery, including necklace and belt-plate (sun-image)
(cf. Tables 14; 15). By contrast, the possibly very young Egtved
woman has short hair, blouse, string skirt, blanket-like wrap,
no dagger, and poor jewellery (no necklace or lunar-shaped
neck collar). It is suggested that we should ascribe unmarried

status to the Egtved woman, even though string skirts also appear in female graves with daggers and fine jewellery, such as Ølby (30-40 years of age) (Fig. 4). At Ølby, the strings of the skirt are even decorated with glistening bronze tubes.

On the same grounds, the young Skrydstrup woman would also have unmarried status. Skrydstrup is likely later than the other graves discussed (Period III C-14 date; cf. Bender Jørgensen, Munksgaard & Stærmose Nielsen 1982, 43f.). The Skrydstrup grave holds very fine garments, including blouse, wrap, and two long plain skirts, as well as golden earrings, the latter no doubt placing her among the high aristocracy or royal families. Strangely, Skrydstrup lacks bronzes. No explanation comes readily to mind; she was probably not a member of a cult group. At Skrydstrup one would have expected at least bracelets, which are found even in children's graves (cf. Willroth 1989).

An important aspect to be considered is secret knowledge. This is demonstrated in the form of calendar systems, hidden in the numbers of spirals of various decorative zones on the fine female belt-plates (as on the sun-disc of the famous model Sun-chariot). Other belt-plates are common imitations, like the ones from Egtved, Borum Eshøj, Tårnholm, and Ølby, the latter perhaps a secondary candidate for high calendar accuracy and cosmological knowledge (Randsborg & Christensen 2006, 99f.; Tables V-VI) (Tables 5-6). Notably, the latter grave also held bossed tutuli and even a rare exotic glass bead, signalling high rank as well as wealth. It is very interesting that certain women carried such superb astronomical knowledge in their bronze images of the sun. It underlines their role in society, and in particular in the sun cult. Notably, we have virtually no male parallels to the belt-plates, only general allusions to the cosmology in the form of decorative spirals and concentric circles, etc., for instance on the handles of swords.

In several high-ranking female graves, such as Borum Eshøj – an old women – and Hesselagergård (AK 2011;B; Sehested 1884, 50f.), necklaces or neck collars were found together with belt-plates, tutuli, bracelets, daggers and fibulae. Another rich grave at Hesselagergård (Sehested 1884, 54f.; AK 2014;A) held belt-plate, fibula and glass beads, in addition to spiral bracelets, but no dagger, or necklace, or neck collar: an unmarried woman with cultic obligations, according to present suggestions (cf. Table 14). Incidentally, the two Hesselager women were buried in respectively early April/early September and early March/mid-October according to the orientation of their coffins.

The fibulae of the women at Hesselagergård were found at the skull, possibly connected with a second skirt. The position is the same as one of the fibulae at the above Melhøj grave (Bender Jørgensen, Munksgaard & Stærmose Nielsen 1982). Certain female graves, like Skrydstrup and Vester Såby of Period III (Tables 5-6), held gold, but no bronze jewellery. The former interment is likely of a rich young woman without cultic obligations (no belt-plate or tutuli), the latter probably the same, but here a string skirt was present, likely because of the time of year. A Period III grave, also with a string skirt, from Store Købinge in Skåne (Scania), held gold and bracelets, plus a few insignificant bronzes: another high-ranking woman without cultic obligations, according to the present scheme.

The suggested criteria for female and male statuses and occupations are, as indicated, listed in Tables 14-15, all based on artefact identification, mainly from graves (cf. Randsborg & Christensen 2006). A few burials have indicators that have not yet been discussed, like medical doctor/surgeon (surgical instruments) (e.g. Broholm 1943-49, III Grave 414; Stjernquist 1961, Pl. XXXIX,3: both of Period IV) and metal craftsman (tools of the craft) (cf. Randsborg 1984). Charioteers are identified by their steering sticks for the horses, usually in the form of bronze points; sometimes the sticks have decorated sockets, even with large ornamental discs, or the 'point' has the shape of a narrow thrusting axe (cf. Kaul & Randsborg 2008; Randsborg 2010).

A double grave from Nordby in Slesvig (Schleswig) held one man with a flange-hilted sword only, a fine fighting weapon, and another male with a gilded all-metal-hilted sword, plus an axe and two lances (to be worked from the chariot?), several other bronzes etc., a bronze-studded wooden cup, and an all-metal steering stick (AK 2538;A-B) (Kaul & Randsborg 2008). We ought here to be dealing with a royal personage accompanied by his high-ranking follower, or body-guard. According to the distribution of the grave goods in the burial, the king was himself driver of the chariot, as was the Pharaoh in many contemporary Egyptian representations.

4.4 Symbols

A peculiar observation needs to be highlighted, namely the inclusion in the Egtved grave of the cremated bones of a 5/6-year-old child, too old to have been the offspring of the main occupant of the coffin. The bones were wrapped in a piece of cloth about 0.2 m^2 in size (Table 9). Folded once, this would have been the same size as the above mentioned sanitary napkins from Skrydstrup and Borum Eshøj (the old woman). This being the case, an extra symbolic dimension is added to this find of a burial inside a burial. The child is possibly a sacrifice, since cremations are extremely rare in the period of the Egtved grave (Period II). Perhaps the dead child was cremated in Late Bronze Age style to aid its ascent to the spiritual world (cf. Kaul 2004, 183f.). The bone bundle with the cremated bones was placed at the shinbones of the Egtved woman, exactly over a cut exit-hole in the bottom of the oak-coffin.

Such 'soul-holes' have also been found in the bottom of other coffins; in a single case an inverted 'funnel' of stone was constructed in and under the stone bed for the oak-coffin (Boye 1896, 46f.). The holes are often taken to have been there to allow body fluids to escape the coffin, but since the whole core of the mound, including the coffin, was drenched in water, this cannot be the case. Interestingly, the rock-carvings on the circle of oblique slabs in an Early Bronze Age mound at Saga-holm, southern Sweden, were meant to be read from below ground, supposedly by spirits, since the graves in the burial mounds were placed on the surface or even higher in the mound (Randsborg 1993, 89f.).

A few of the cremated bones of the child were deliberately deposited in the same box as the items belonging to the supposed sanitary napkin. Thus a link between the child and the sanitary napkin is a possibility. It would seem that the sanitary napkin is an accentuation of the non-pregnant status, even virginity, of the Egtved woman, while the small, supposedly sacrificed, child carries a reference to what she did not attain – status as a married woman and mother. The sacrifice is offensive to some modern sentiment, but would not be to a West African, for example. Indeed, all 'towels' may be viewed as symbols of virginity when found with young women. Only in the case of the woman from Borum Eshøj, another explanation should be forwarded: a breechcloth for the elderly lady, likely suffering from illnesses of the abdomen.

A symbolic parallel is the young man from Borum Eshøj, who carries a wooden sword scabbard (Boye 1896, 55f.) (Table 7). The weapon in the scabbard is not the fine sword of a commander, but a short simple dagger befitting a young man. The symbolic implications are that the young man, about 20 years of age, was supposed to have obtained a higher rank, likely rather soon, but his 'biography' was cut short by an early death. In accordance with the dagger, the young man was buried without a fully grown fighter's war cap. He was even lacking in foot-wraps, and thus in footwear. Thus, footwear, present in the Egtved grave of a member of a cult group, also carries information on adult social status.

By contrast to the young man at Borum Eshøj, the life of other dead persons from the Early Bronze Age was seemingly fulfilled, in spite of their death at a relatively young age, as was common in Prehistory, not least for women (Randsborg & Christensen 2006). The implication is that all the elements of the graves should be considered 'symbolic', due and according to their cultural content and pertaining phenotypes. Functional and social aspects are important too, of course, like the warmth and status of a garment, the efficiency and importance of a weapon, and, for the jewellery – roles and status. A razor is not just a razor, but also a statement on male appearance, at least in death, as confirmed by the clean-shaven faces of the princes in the oak-coffin graves.

Some symbolic items, pertaining to a traditional definition of the concept, are nevertheless difficult to interpret, like the mysterious five small stones in the male oak-coffin grave in Lille Dragshøj, or the six flat hazel sticks in the male Guldhøj grave (game or divination?) (Boye 1896, 75; 116, with Pl. XV:16-17).

Taken together, these observations imply that seemingly insignificant items and small details may carry a particular and profound meaning in connection with the burial of these prominent personages of the distant late second millennium BC, so far back in time that analogies may have lost their significance – almost.

5

Europe and Beyond

5.1 Parallels

The earlier European Bronze Age seems to display a 'faultline' as regards the use of materials for textiles (cf. Chapter 1 and §2.1 above; Bender Jørgensen 1992, 116f. with Fig. 140; Grömer 2006, 52f.). Generally, the textile finds to the north and east of a line from the lowermost Rhine to Bavaria and Austria, then south to the head of the Adriatic Sea, are in wool, those to the west of this line in linen. Observations are few (except for Denmark) and variations in preservation always a factor: woollen textiles may have been present in areas and finds with linens; also, linen is often more poorly preserved than wool. Nevertheless, the geographical distinction may be significant when discussing European parallels to the magnificent Danish Bronze Age textiles and related questions. In the Neolithic, linen is also found in eastern Germany (as well as in the Baltic region) (Bender Jørgensen 1992, 114f. with Fig. 139). In the Iron Age linen occurs widely to the south and south-east of Denmark.

The Nordic Early Bronze Age wool garments for both women and men seem to have had contemporary parallels in the North Alpine area to the south of Denmark, even if such have not been preserved, except for small fragments of textiles (cf. Bender Jørgensen 1986; 1992). A female blouse or T-shirt is revealed by small added-on bronze sheet metal tutuli in Period II graves from the Lüneburg area of Niedersachsen (Lower Saxony) (Piesker 1958, Taf. 66). Slightly later finds (Period III) come from Lübz (Sprockhoff 1939; Herrmann 1989, 95; Wels-Weyrauch 1994, 61 Abb. 56A) (Fig. 30), and Thürgow in

Mecklenburg. It has been suggested that the latter garments were in fact leather capes, at Thügow also decorated with normal tutuli with a point (Schmidt 2007; Scherping & Schmidt 2007). In the Thürgow grave, textiles of (likely) wild silk also appeared – a strong indication of long-distance foreign contacts and exchange of cloth (Schmidt 2004; 2007; Scherping & Schmidt 2007; Randsborg & Christensen 2006, 25f.). Decorated bonnets are revealed by patterns of added-on sheet metal tutuli and other bronzes in Period II graves from the Lüneburg area (cf. Piesker 1958, 18f.; with Abb. 4-5).

The Thürgow grave also contained a neck-collar of a particular Mecklenburg type. Female bronzes rarely transgress the cultural boundaries of well-defined sub-areas (unlike male weapons, drinking vessels, etc.). Significantly, such collars have also been found in graves in Holsten (Holstein) and on the Jylland (Jutland) peninsula, likely revealing patterns of directional high ranking exogamic marriages. Such 'exchanges' occur at landward distances of up to about 200 km, and likely more by sea (Schmidt 2007, 97 Abb. 13; Jockenhövel 1991). If persons with neck-collars 'travel', textiles would have done the same.

From the Netherlands (Holland) comes a bog-body found at Emmer-Erfscheienveen, dated to *c*. 1300 BC (Fig. 29). The person, evidently a man, is primarily dressed in hide and fur of sheep (cap), calf (cloak), and deer (shoes), but wore a poorly preserved woollen coat (Vons-Comis 1990; van der Sanden 1996). The find is particularly interesting in demonstrating outer garments made of hide and fur. Coats of hide were no doubt also worn. The find emphasises that full woven woollen textiles were for the elites.

Attempts at reconstructing female dresses, though only in outline, have been based on graves at Werra River in Thüringen (Thuringia), Central Germany; Werra empties into the Weser River and ultimately into the North Sea at Bremen (Feustel 1958, cf. 50f.; Farke 1993). These graves, contemporary with the Nordic Period II milieu, are rich in female jewellery and also hold fragments of textiles. The quality of the cloth, as measured by number threads per cm, is clearly higher than in the North; this being the case particularly for light and open 'veil' cloth, a highly remarkable product (Table 16). The Thüringen cloths, nearly all in S/S spinning, would seem to indicate that the contemporary coarser Nordic textiles were locally produced. Of two woollen textile fragments in S/S spinning from Unterteutschenthal near Halle in the same general region, dated to the local 'Early Bronze Age' (close of the Stone Age in the North), the one with the weft in plant fibres also displays a high number of threads per cm (Schlabow 1959, 118f.). A few woollen textiles from Lower Saxony and Mecklenburg (Nordic Periods II-III) are also of a relatively high quality, but uncertainty reigns since the dress items involved are unknown.

A short skirt, likely a string skirt, seems to be present in Oberbayern (Upper Bavaria), again revealed by added-on small tutuli of bronze found in a female grave (Naue 1894, 39f.; 271f. & Taf. VII; with XIX & XX; cf. Broholm & Hald 1939, 97 Fig. 219) (Fig. 31). Reconstructing the skirt as a long plain one, with the bronze decoration merely applied to the upper part, is possible, but rather unlikely. There are also other candidates for string skirts from South Germany (Wels-Weyrauch 1989, 124 Abb. 4B; 127 Abb. 7A).

The western Alpine area sees some of the earliest preserved textiles and garments in other materials than wool, particularly in linen. Finds in tabby from Neolithic Switzerland are well known (Vogt 1937; Drack 1969/R. Wyss, 136f. with 134 Abb. 15; Stöckli, Niffeler & Gross-Klee 1995, 169f./A. Rast-Eicher). Parallels come from northernmost Italy, including a 2 m long, quite narrow patterned linen textile from Molina di Ledro (Barbar 1991, 174f. with Fig. 6.4; Gleba 2008, 43). By far the most important find of early garments belongs to the so-called 'Ice Man' from Ötztal in the eastern Alps, about 40 years of age at death and dated to about 3300 BC (e.g. Höpfel, Platzer & Spindler 1992 and following; Egg & Spindler 2009; websites include Wikipedia's Ötzi the Iceman and iceman.it of the Südtüroler Archäologiemuseum, Bozen).

5. Europe and Beyond

The body and clothing of the Ice Man are very well preserved, including sophisticated items in leather and fur and a protective matting of woven grass. The main garment is a large, probably sleeved and no doubt belted, coat in lengths of alternating dark and light goat's hide. A very long belt holds a pouch with various items. Leggings, also in goatskin, are supported by a garter belt arrangement; a breechcloth is in the same material. Heavy shoes have a grass netting frame with hay, they are in deerskin with bearskin soles and were perhaps snowshoes; a bearskin cap completes the dress. The pattern of the goat-skin coat somewhat resembles the female blouses or T-shirts of the North in the Bronze Age, again pointing to their potentially great age as an item of dress.

The western Alpine regions displays examples of large steles of the Late Neolithic depicting humans in various belted dresses and with jewellery and weapons (Drack 1969/R. Wyss, 152 with 148f. Abb. 12-13; Stöckli, Niffeler & Gross-Klee 1995, 250f. with Abb. 153/P. Moinat & W.E. Stöckli). These steles are some of the earliest representations of human beings in temperate Europe after the Ice Age; clearly a new interest in the individual, no doubt members of the elite, characterises the third millennium BC. This interest, predicting Bronze Age behaviour, was linked with social display in terms of both artefacts and clothing.

Numerous large fragments of Middle Bronze Age textiles come from the salt works at Hallstatt in Austria (Grömer 2006; 2007). The textiles, like the Nordic ones, are in simple woollen tabby (apart from a couple in linen). There are interesting details, like different edges and colouring, and the cloth is fine (Table 17). A few very early examples of twill are noteworthy. There are several spinning combinations including the S/S of Thüringen, but Z-combinations are the most common. Incidentally, a pointed Late Bronze Age leather cap with tassels also comes from the Hallstatt mines (Probst 1996, 383); an earlier cap (or rather helmet) of osier comes from Fiavé-Carera, Northern Italy (Randsborg 1993, 114 Fig. 61).

A number of grave- and other finds from the same overall

95

region confirm this picture. Interestingly, textiles in linen are particularly impressive. A famous piece of embroidery in linen from Switzerland has recently been redated from the Neolithic to about 1600 BC, or the local Middle Bronze Age (cf. Grömer 2006, 43f. Abb. 13). A large woollen blanket of 2.0x1.7 m ($5^{1}\!2$ feet wide, area of 3.4 m²) from a late Early Bronze Age grave at Pustopolje in Bosnia-Herzegovina (contemporary with the beginning of the Nordic Early Bronze Age) is promising news, which can be supplemented (Grömer 2006, 45 Abb. 15).

South and southeast of the Alps, knowledge of early dress comes in particular from images. The earliest clay figurines are Neolithic in date, followed by evocative Copper Age human beings, mostly women (Gimbutas 1982; Merkyte 2005, 95f. with Plates 18-19; Hansen 2007, with massive amounts of data). These interesting figurines display naked painted or tattooed figures, masked persons, and a number of variously dressed human beings, mainly females (Gimbutas 1982, 44f. with Figs 1ff.). Among the dress items are ornamental belts resting on the hips, sometimes with tassels recalling the string skirts of a much later Nordic Bronze Age. Long skirts and tightly fitting blouses also occur; shoes, coiffures and caps are noted.

Female figurines from the Balkan Bronze Age, apart from rich jewellery, also indicate the existence of tightly fitting blouses (T-shirts), belts and long voluminous skirts, perhaps inspired from the Aegean, patterned with embroidery, and sometimes even with aprons (cf. Müller-Karpe 1980, Vol. IV;3, Taf. 326, with Taf. 282 & 327; Schumacher-Matthäus 1985; cf. Dumitrescu 1961) (Fig. 32). Footwear does not appear on these representations. The suggestion that the said figurines represent men is in all likelihood wrong.

In Late Bronze Age Greece, a female blouse (T-shirt), or rather tightly fitting very short-sleeved decorated jacket with an open front – consciously exposing the breasts – is common. (Strangely, such a jacket was worn by Greek men until recent times (Riis 1993, 174 Fig. 121).) With the blouse come finely decorated long voluminous skirts with horizontal pleats and

occasionally an apron (Müller-Karpe 1980, e.g. Taf. 251; Marinatos 1960, Pl. XXIV; Fig. 160). From Aegean wall-paintings it
appears that female clothing was very colourful, and that the
women in all likelihood were using cosmetics. This is in stark
contrast to contemporary Nordic garments that seem to come
only in variations of brown and occasionally white. Only the
colours of bronze and gold jewellery, and perhaps a few amber
or glass beads, added other hues to the skin and hair of the
Nordic woman: a highly conscious simplicity, though hardly
modesty. The metal alone would speak of wealth and foreign
contact. The simplicity is strange, but also interesting, since
embroidery is one of the arts truly mastered in the Nordic
Early Bronze Age, but never applied for conspicuous ornamental decoration of garments.

Men in Bronze Age Greece are depicted with only a loincloth,
or wearing a very large cloak (Müller-Karpe 1980, Taf. 218;
255). The loincloths may even open like shorts (Marinatos
1960, Pl. XXXVI, below). Late Bronze Age warriors wore a
tightly fitting long-sleeved blouse (possibly with a leather cui-
rass), short frilled loincloth, leggings and leather sandals
(Marinatos 1960, Pl. 232-3). Leather and bronze body-armour
occurs from Central Europe to the Aegean in the last centuries
of the second millennium BC. Male 'barbarian' opponents,
dressed only in fur coats, also appear, no doubt representing an
early idea of 'the other' as primitive and wild, and quite different from the European aristocratic *koinê*. The latter shaped the
core parts of Europe in the Bronze Age, and certainly Denmark
as well, from a Late Stone Age basis of regional differences and
alternative life-ways.

Special clothing for ritual performances is also seen, such as
long fur skirts for both men and women (Marinatos 1960, Pls
XXVII-XXX). Very many interesting details are known, including tall and beautiful female coiffures (Marinatos 1960, Figs
16-17). Footwear is rare in the representations and seemingly
mostly (only?) worn by men (as warriors), often in the form of
boots (leggings?), or sandals. Women are probably mainly depicted indoors, in palaces and homes, or participating in

ceremonies, while the men are both at ceremonies and out-doors, for instance travelling or fighting. The Greek Late Bronze Age also provides much written evidence on professional groups of textile producers, in particular concerning distribution of wool and weaving (e.g. Ventris & Chadwick 1956; cf. §2.3 above).

In conclusion, we see evidence of tightly fitting blouses (T-shirts) and long skirts for women across Europe from north to south. Wraps were also in use. String skirts are unknown in the Aegean, where women may bare their breasts but not their legs. After 1000 BC, knowledge of dress fashion in the Mediterranean is much greater as a result of very many pictorial representations (Kastelic 1965; Frey 1969; Gleba 2008). Newly found whole textiles comprise large magnificent cloaks and a coat from a royal tomb (with a throne) at Verucchio, northern Central Italy, dated to the eighth century BC (e.g. Elis 2002; Gleba 2008, 49 Fig. 29, with references). The central part of the back of the wooden throne carries images of giant looms, stressing the importance of textile production for the early Italian Iron Age. Complete leggings and socks are found at Vedretta di Ries in northernmost Italy, dated to between 800 and 500 BC (Gleba 2008, 47 Fig. 27).

Sadly, this just about exhausts the information we have from Europe on parallels to the unique complete woollen garments preserved in the North.

5.2 Exchange

Bronze Age exchange, even over considerable distances, is clearly demonstrated by the patterns of artefact distribution established by European and Near Eastern archaeology across almost two centuries of research. Exchange at shorter distances comes as no surprise. Exchange over longer distances requires a particular energy, in particular if it is directional and not just an accumulated sequence of short-distance exchanges. As to Europe, virtually no contemporary documents can help us. But the Near East may inspire, especially concerning high-ranking directional exchange, such as is described in the Bible.

Arriving at Jerusalem with a very great caravan – with camels carrying spices, large quantities of gold, and precious stones – she came to Solomon [died *c.* 931 BC] and talked with him about all that she had on her mind. When the queen of Sheba saw all the wisdom of Solomon and the palace he had built, the food on his table, the seating of his officials, the attending servants in their robes, his cupbearers, and the burnt offerings he made at the temple of the Lord, she was overwhelmed. And she gave the king 120 talents [4½ tons] of gold, large quantities of spices, and precious stones. Never again were so many spices brought in as those the queen of Sheba gave to King Solomon. King Solomon gave the queen of Sheba all she desired and asked for, besides what he had given her out of his royal bounty. Then she left and returned with her retinue to her own country.

King Solomon made two hundred large shields of hammered gold; six hundred bekas [3.5 kg] of gold went into each shield. He also made three hundred small shields of hammered gold, with three minas [1.7 kg] of gold in each shield. The king put them in the Palace of the Forest of Lebanon. Then the king made a great throne inlaid with ivory and overlaid with fine gold. All King Solomon's goblets were of gold, and all the household articles in the Palace of the Forest of Lebanon were pure gold. The king had a fleet of trading ships at sea. Once every three years it returned, carrying gold, silver and ivory, and apes and baboons.

King Solomon was greater in riches and wisdom than all the other kings of the earth. Year after year, everyone who came brought a gift – articles of silver and gold, robes, weapons and spices, and horses and mules. Solomon accumulated chariots and horses; he had fourteen hundred chariots and twelve thousand horses, which he kept in the chariot cities and also with him in Jerusalem. The King made silver as common in Jerusalem as stone, and cedar as plentiful as sycamore-fig trees in the foothills. Solomon's horses were imported from Egypt and from Kue [Cilicia?]. They imported a chariot from Egypt for six hundred shekels of silver [7 kg], and a horse for a hundred and fifty [1.7 kg]. They also exported them to all the kings of the Hittites and of the Arameans.

I Kings 10, abbreviated extracts

Bronze Age archaeology instructs us that male items are both 'regional' and 'supra-regional' in their cultural geography, female ones merely 'sub-regional' and 'regional': only travelling further through marriages (or by particular male linkages). Men were likely in charge of foreign contacts, including metal and other trade, even though women would have been important agents, in particular concerning textiles. In the Late Bronze Age, Nordic artefacts – both male and female ones – could travel very far north, but rarely went further south than a line running Groningen – Dortmund – Leipzig – Berlin – Szczecin (Stettin) – (possibly) Gdansk (Danzig) (Thrane 1975a, 231 Fig. 148) (Fig. 28). This line corresponds to a marriage-defined contact zone of about 200 km, in this case, south (and east) of the Nordic Bronze Age culture zone (cf. §5.1). In the Early Bronze Age zone this was restricted to areas north of the lowermost Elbe, in the Late Bronze Age to areas north of the lower Elbe regions. The north German regions in question were living under the 'spell' of the North, copying Nordic norms in the making of their own artefacts.

Only a few Nordic Late Bronze Age artefacts travelled further south, among these both male and female ones (Fig. 28). Perhaps most of this traffic was in scrap metal and determined by demand in the southern regions. A huge Late Bronze Age deposit from Vénat, south-western France, contained 2,800 bronzes (75 kg), most from western France, but many from the North, the British Isles, Central Europe, Spain, Sardinia and

Sicily (Coffyn, Gomez & Mohen 1981); three-quarters of the items were scrap metal.

Studies of archaeological networks in Central Europe indicate that materials for jewellery in the Upper Palaeolithic might have been collected from more than 500 km away, and Early Neolithic (Linear Ceramic culture) materials from almost 2,000 km away, though probably not by one and the same agent (Jöris 2008, 122 Abb. 55). On this perspective, Bronze Age transportation of both materials and finished products over long distances is nothing to wonder at. The question is rather the character of the exchange and the number of long-distance personal contacts.

Only very rarely do grave finds from Central Europe display Nordic bronzes, such as the case of Late Bronze Age Kapusany in north-eastern Slovakia (Jockenhövel 1971, 202f.; Taf. 29, 386; Novotná 1980, 141f.; Taf. 42:941). This male cremation contains a razor with S-shaped handle of Nordic type, tweezers (which might also be Nordic), an awl, a fragment of a small ring, and a pin which is probably of Lusitanian (or Lausitz) type (East Central Europe). The find probably represents an ordinary traveller arriving from the North. A Nordic razor of Early Bronze Age Period III has been found in a grave in Moravia; from the same region come several Nordic bronzes of the same date (Jockenhövel 1971, 200f.; Taf. 29:385). In a southeasterly direction, Nordic Late Bronze Age bronzes, even a mould, have been found as far away as Romania (Thrane 1975a, 223f.). From the area of the sanctuary of Dodona in northwestern Greece seemingly comes a pair of Nordic Late Bronze Age tweezers (Period IV) (Carapanos 1878, 95 no. 11; Pl. LI:21, perhaps even LI:20).

By contrast, the North, apart from metallic raw materials, received a surprising amount of Danubian luxury items (e.g. Thrane 1975a, Figs 81, 89, and 95). Metal-rich Central Europe may have admired the organisational skills and technology of the North, the latter comprising fine structures and housing, elegant light and fast boats, capable of covering long distances quickly, supreme casting of beautiful bronzes, and manufacture of simple elegant clothing (cf. Randsborg & Christensen 2006, 59ff.).

In the Baltic and the North Sea, superb seafaring technology, along with military prowess, would have secured 'Danish' supremacy. But such cannot easily be extended southwards along the rivers of the Continent, except by well established social networks and extraordinary trading goods. Locally available amber is not much used in the North during the Early Bronze Age; it is also rather uncommon in Central Europe, but does occur as far south as the Mediterranean and at ancient Qatna in western Syria (Harding & Hughes-Brock 1974). Amber alone cannot explain the massive import of metals to the North, as was once believed; rather amber was an auxiliary source of income, like a number of other items. If a major source is looked for, it is rather textiles, as will be argued below, even though Nordic cloth was rather coarse.

Still, it would seem that the balance of exchange, especially in metals, is tipped so much in favour of the Nordic Bronze Age, especially the early part, that social and ideological factors must also be considered in understanding the particular prestige of the North. One may, for instance, point to a highly developed cosmology, including calendar knowledge, important sacred sites, and lavish ritual performances (Randsborg 1993; Randsborg & Christensen 2006, 59ff.; Kaul 2004). The North is also the awe-inspiring land of the never-setting sun in the summer, and the never-rising sun in the winter, and, therefore a key on earth for understanding the mysteries of the universe.

Already in the Early Bronze Age, valuable ideologically loaded European cult items and high status symbols of power travelled to the North, and vice versa. A divine oversized axe, made in the North, is found in Belgium, perhaps together with a Nordic spearhead (Kaul 1991). A Hungarian cosmological drum is found as far north as Skåne (Scania) (Randsborg & Christensen 2006, 62f.). A western French cult sword (Briard 1965, 91f. with Fig. 28), possibly from Brittany, travelled, perhaps by way of the Netherlands or even England, to Jylland (Jutland) (AK 10; 4704). A similar item has recently come to

102

light at Oxborough, Norfolk (British Museum PE 1994,1003.1). The heaviest gold artefact of the Early Bronze Age in Denmark, an English bracelet, travelled to Sjælland (Zealand), despite very little other contact across the North Sea in those days (DB I, 331 c2; DB II, 159 Pl. 12; 160). In the Late Bronze Age, a lur trumpet, likely made on Sjælland, travelled to Latvia (Broholm, Larsen & Skjerne 1949, 34). In particular, the otherwise uncommon western connections are remarkable. If fine metal artefacts travelled, fine textiles would have done the same, as well as other items.

Such travel is probably the result of very special occasions, journeys undertaken to holy sites and powerful leaders in connection with ritual and social events. In the North, such sites are exemplified by sacred rocks with rock carvings; it is imagined that local princely households would have accommodated the foreigners (for perspective, see Kristiansen & Larsson 2005). Long-distance traffic of this character would also have been aimed at social matters and common exchanges, in much the same way as the Biblical account of the tenth-century BC journey by the Queen of Sheba to King Solomon of Israel, quoted at the start of this chapter. In the Biblical journey, a queen is performing the role of a male ruler. The same chapters in the Bible also give an interesting (although wildly exaggerated) account of royal magnificence, performance, and munificence at the time of the Nordic early Late Bronze Age, as well as of the types of artefacts involved and their importance.

An alternative explanation of the many foreign artefacts in the Nordic Bronze Age, including all the metal, is that the North travelled south, even to Central Europe, to acquire the said prestigious items, plus the metal, foreign textiles, glass beads, etc. This is altogether possible, but often disregarded as a hypothesis, seemingly on the assumption that the North was always a passive receiving partner, and that there ought to have been further common cultural elements. But this need not be the case, since demonstration of cultural 'independence' is an important social signature. Furthermore, there is no archaeological problem in suggesting that the North was active in relation to the huge northern parts of Scandinavia. It is also argued that travels may primarily have been to areas defined by the limits of the loose southern scatter of Nordic items, and not further south, to the mining areas (Fig. 28).

This being said, plundering for metals and other valuable items cannot be ruled out, even though it is an uncertain method. The Danish region was populous and well-equipped with fast boats. Plundering northern neighbours would not have been very rewarding (except as to textiles, perhaps), but the southern Baltic coast would constitute a target, as Lithuanian artefacts in Denmark may reveal (Sidrys & Luchtanas 1999, cf. 171 Fig. 4). In such a case, distance may actually reward 'irresponsible' behaviour. Coastal plundering is also less dangerous than expeditions over land. Expeditions along the European rivers cannot be ruled out, for instance in connection with social visits gone awry, but would be dangerous since the escape route can easily be blocked. In fact, 'Viking rules' would also apply to Bronze Age warfare.

In the Early Bronze Age, an international understanding of the importance and significance of fast chariots and boats, thrones (folding stools), fine drinking vessels, weapons (shields, swords and spears), raw-materials such as copper, tin, gold, and other exotica (at least for the North), was common. Added to this are advanced cosmological knowledge and calendars, foreign textiles, etc. Among other finds, the huge and extraordinary Kivig (Kivik) ('Ki Cove') cairn dating from the transition between Periods II and III, with its fantastic picture programme, shows evidence of this environment as well as truly long-distance travel, possibly even to the Near East (Randsborg 1993).

Strangely, 'Ki' is ancient Sumerian for the Earth (etc.), or the Earth god. The basic elements of the Sumerian universe, as no doubt also of the Nordic Bronze Age one, are earth, sky and sea. The huge Kivig cairn is deliberately positioned between these elements, not on top of a hill as is common in the Early Nordic Bronze Age. Ultra-short place names, like many names of islands, supposedly have a long ancestry, likely older than the Iron Age. Perhaps the Kivig grave even held a King 'Ki' of 1300 BC: a Nordic Gilgamesh, even though a Nordic Odysseus also comes to mind, as a big man from a small place.

The famous Mesopotamian (Early) Bronze Age Epic of Gilgamesh, King of the city of Uruk, may also be evoked in this context, including some archaeologically recognisable items, also present in the Biblical accounts of King Solomon. Travel and knowledge of the world, as always, play a large and status-giving role (Sandars 1960, prose edition):

And now they brought to them the weapons, they put in their hands the great swords in their golden scabbards, and the bow and the quiver. Gilgamesh took the axe ... and your chariot horses shall be famous far-off for their swiftness.

As for you, Gilgamesh, ... Let your clothes be fresh, bathe yourself in water, cherish the little child that holds your hand, and make your wife happy in your embrace; for this too is the lot of man.

... the king, who knew the countries of the world. He was wise, he saw mysteries and knew secret things, he brought us a tale of the days before the flood. He went on a long journey, was weary, worn out with labour, and returning engraved on a stone the whole story. ... In nether-earth the darkness will show him a light: of man-kind, all that are known, none will leave a monument for generations to come to compare with his.

Epic of Gilgamesh, abbreviated extracts

5.3 The balance of trade

Looking at prices of commodities and services, and even of other entities, such as fines, an interesting picture emerges as to the value of textiles in the Eastern Mediterranean and adjacent areas for the centuries parallel to the Nordic Early Bronze Age. An Aegean Linear B text from Pylos seems to indicate a rather high value of 1 kg of bronze for a tunic of fine linen. Another textile, likely quite small, costs only 45 g of bronze, while an over-shirt also has the value of 1 kg of bronze (Ventris & Chadwick 1956, Tablet 222). Unfortunately, these prices cannot be juxtaposed with values of other commodities.

Hittite laws, however, are copious as regards prices and related matters (Hoffner 1997; cf. Bryce 2002) (Table 18). A Hittite shekel weighs 11.75 g, a mina (40 shekels) 470 g. Prices are stated in silver shekels, and seem high overall, even though exchanges were basically in commodities rather than in metal. The ratio between silver and worked copper may have been about 1:57, to judge from the fact that 12.5 silver shekels is the price of a copper box weighing 1.5 minas (Law 160; in Hoffner 1997). Copper as a commodity seems much cheaper: Law 181 gives the price of 4 minas of copper (= 160 shekels in weight, or 1880 g) for only 1 silver shekel. Simple copper artefacts are also cheap: a copper axe of one mina (470 g) costs 0.125 of a silver shekel, while a bronze axe of 2 minas (940 g) costs 0.33 shekels.

Compared to these prices, animals are expensive, from a sheep valued at 1 silver shekel to a cow at 7, a bull at 10, a plough ox at 12, a draft horse at 20, and even a mule at 40 silver shekels. Food prices seem reasonable but are slightly confusing. 200 litres of barley is 0.5 silver shekel, the same as one (big?) cheese, and the meat of one ox; 150 litres of wheat is 1 silver shekel. Garments and other such items are very costly indeed. A fine sheet is 15 silver shekels, a large bolt of linen is 5, while various garments are given as 3-12 silver shekels; a blue woollen garment is as high as 20 silver shekels. A sheepskin with fleece is 1 and the hide of an ox 1-4 silver shekels.

If temperate Europe, or some other region like the Aegean, was delivering textiles or even animals to the Hittites (the latter is hardly likely), the prices in metal obtained in Anatolia would have been very handsome indeed. Hittite prices may even suggest that that textiles usually considered 'homespun', and thus cheap, were also quite costly in the Nordic Early Bronze Age.

Contemporary New Kingdom Egypt is another region that

yields copious data on prices, etc. (Janssen 1975) (Table 19). The standard unit is the 91 g deben; a smaller unit is a tenth of a deben, the kit, at 9.4 g = 80% of the 11.8 g Hittite silver shekel. The approximate ratio between gold, silver and copper is 1:2:200. Prices are usually stated in copper deben. Metal artefacts and other items are not particularly cheap: A bronze jar at 1.6 silver kit = 18 copper deben, a bronze cup is 5 copper deben, a big spear is 2 (a normal one is 1.5), a leather bucket is 3, and a basket is 4.

Animals are priced as follows: a goat 2.5 copper deben, a donkey 25-40, an ox 60, a bull 50-120, and a cow up to 140. Food prices seems reasonable, a sack of wheat (*c.* 58 kg) stands at 1-2 copper deben (barley being perhaps slightly more expensive), a loaf of bread at 0.1, 50 fish at 2, and the thigh of a cow at *c.* 30 copper deben; a litre of beer is rather expensive at 0.5 copper deben. Again, garments seem quite costly, even if made only of linen (Egypt did not appreciate wool, likely for climatic reasons, but a taboo could also be argued). Thus a linen sheet is listed at 3.5 silver kit = 33 copper deben, 10 shirts of fine linen at 4 silver kit = 38 copper deben (a single shirt is listed as 2.5-5.0); a 'smooth' garment is 10-30 bronze deben, a pair of sandals 2. Among personal belongings of interest is a razor at 1-2 copper deben, a mirror at 6, and a necklace of glass beads at 5. All this should be compared to the low wages for ordinary people. A slave girl could be acquired for 4 silver deben = 380 copper deben. Furniture was 12-20 copper deben for a bed, 13-20 for a chair, a table was 15. Funerals were costly, though: a burial shroud is listed as 5 silver kit = 50 copper deben, a simple coffin as 20-40, and a scribe's coffin at 200 copper deben; a 'Book of the Dead' (standard magic formulas used at death) is 100 copper deben.

As in the Aegean and in Anatolia with the Hittites, Egypt reveals high prices for clothing, but unlike in the Hittite Kingdom, metal artefacts do not seem particularly cheap. Would the Aegean and related kingdoms have brought metal and cloth to Egypt? They would certainly have been sailing the wine-dark sea with ceramics and other items, in ships loaded with metal

107

vessels, as depicted on Egyptian wall-paintings. The newly found fortress of Avaris in the Nile Delta, with Minoan palatial paintings and emblems, testifies to close contacts between the areas in the sixteenth century BC.

The wreck of Ulu-Burun, off the south-west coast of Turkey, dendro-dated to 1300 BC, was filled with copper and tin ingots, as well as very many other items. The ship also had a couple of Aegean passengers on board and artefacts with Balkan and even more distant origins, like amber from the Baltic. A wreck from the end of the thirteenth century BC, also with a cargo of metal, comes from nearby Cape Gelidonya.

Documents from Ugarit (Ras Shamra) on the Syrian coast are rich in information on prices of various items, even though disagreement reigns as to the readings (Heltzer 1978, incl. 17f.; 73f.; cf. Vargyas 1986; Stieglitz 1979; Mederos & Lamberg-Karlovsky 2001). 1 Ugarit shekel = 9.4 g of silver, or 80% of the 11.75 g Hittite shekel. The gold:silver:tin ratio is seemingly 1:4:800, which makes copper/tin very cheap. The price of a slave woman is given as 13 shekels of gold or 52 of silver; thus copper and bronze seem to have (nearly) the same value as tin. At late third millennium BC Ebla in western Syria, it is claimed, 1 x gold = 7-8 x silver = 56-80 x tin (Burney 2004, 229). 1 parîsu (perhaps 15 litres) of wheat is 1 shekel, while 5 parîsu is the same as one jar of oil. A sheep is 0.6-1 shekel a head, a bull 10 or less, while a mare is 35 shekels. A copper cup is 2 shekels. The price of wool varies according to its quality, untreated wool priced at 2-7 shekels per talent (28.2 kg), woven wool at 5. Dresses vary very much in price, from 25 shekels for a ceremonial garment to 18 for a scarlet one, and about 3.3 for a robe. The cheapest garment priced is 1.5 shekels. Again, textiles are costly.

To round up this discussion of prices in the Bronze Age civilisations, a short survey of prices in Babylon at the time of Hammurabi (1700 BC) should be appended (Meissner 1936). 1 shekel here = 8.4 g of silver; 60 shekels = 1 mina (0.504 kg). The ratio between gold and silver fluctuated around 1:10. The ratio between silver and tin is given as 1:14.5. 1 mina of copper was about 2 silver shekels. A copper kettle was priced at 2 shekels. A slave was about 0.3 mina of silver (168 g, or 20 shekels), or the same as an average cow, a donkey was 16, and a sheep 2 shekels. 5 mina of wool were 5 shekels. Again, textiles were expensive, three woollen garments are priced at 1 shekel of silver, one at 0.5 shekels, and one at 0.8 shekels. A document from 1100 BC gives one woollen shirt at 1 shekel, two old headdresses at 12, and nine cloaks at 18 shekels.

The much later Edict of the Roman Emperor Diocletian (301 AD, incomplete), which set minimum prices, is very detailed regarding services and many commodities, including textiles, which again are costly (Frank 1940, 305ff./E.R. Graser). A *castrensis modius* (CM) equals 1.5 regular modius of 6.5 kg. Thus, 1 CM of wheat (9.75 kg) is 100 denars, while the same measure of barley is 60 denars. An Italian pint (0.273 litre) of beer is 2-4 denars. An Italian pound (336 g) of pork is 12 denars, the same of beef 8 denars, while two chickens are 60 and a fattened goose 200 denars. An Italian pound of sea fish is 24 denars, while the same amount of dried cheese is 12. A CM (9.75 kg) of salt is 100 denars. Some basic foodstuffs are modestly priced, while luxuries carry high prices.

As to wages, a farm labourer, with maintenance, receives 25 denars a day, the same as a scribe for 100 lines of the best writing; a coppersmith earns 6 denars per pound (or 336 g) of small vessels, and a tailor 60 denars for cutting and finishing a hooded cloak of the finest quality, while he earns 100 for a horse blanket of felt (of three pounds, or nearly 1 kg), but only 20 for breeches. A wool weaver, with maintenance, receives 40 denars for working one pound of wool; a good linen weaver receives the same by day. Fulling of textiles is labour-intensive, thus rather expensive: fulling of a new light cloak is 50 denars.

A soldier's woollen mantle of the best quality is 4,000 denars, while a common hooded cloak of wool is 4,500 denars; a Gallic shirt of wool is 1,250 denars; a cover of the best quality (for a bed) is 1,600 denars (white wool of 12 pounds, or *c.* 4 kg). A linen shirt of the first (best) quality for soldiers is 1,500 denars. One Babylonian (ox) hide of first quality is 500 denars while a sheep skin for a cap is 100 denars (best quality). Incidentally, this is the same as one pound of goose down. A seal skin is a high 1,250 denars, while the hide of a lion is only 1,000. A pound (336 g) of white silk is 12,000 denars (the same amount of purple dyed silk being a very high 150,000 denars), while the same amount of the best 'middle quality' washed wool is 50 denars. One pound of gold (336 g) stands at 50,000 denars. Unfortunately, the Edict, despite including a surprising number of commodity details, is incomplete and does not tell us much about metals.

5.4 A theory about the Bronze Age

Observations on prices of textiles and other commodities in the East Mediterranean civilisations give rise to an embracing theory about the Bronze Age, both in the North and in other regions of Europe (Tables 17-18). The balance of trade between foodstuffs, animals, domestic everyday items and even luxury products is usually in favour of textiles, to judge by the prices. The production of textiles demands much labour, but this is exactly what Europe and the North had plenty of in the Bronze Age. Thus, highly priced textiles would have been a prime commodity, in particular for regions with no gold, tin or copper. This is not to say that Denmark exported textiles to Babylon; the claim is merely one of direction – textiles for important commodities. Thus, Denmark may primarily have exported textiles to the northern German area with many Nordic arte-facts (cf. Fig. 28). In turn, Denmark may have received textiles and wool from northern parts of Scandinavia. The south-eastern Baltic bronzes found in Denmark may even have been payment for woollen textiles from a region with mostly linen garments, rather than plundered goods brought home by 'Danes' from marauding expeditions.

Baltic amber has been seen as a prized commodity in Central Europe and the Mediterranean, which no doubt it was, but it is questionable whether the rather small amounts recorded would have sufficed to pay for the large quantities of gold and bronze that arrived in the North (Harding & Hughes-Brock 1974). Regularity of supply is another issue. In Greece, amber is rather plentiful at the beginning of the Late Bronze Age (the seventeeth to fifteenth centuries BC), in particular at the palaces of Mycenae and Pylos (Manning et al. 2006). Amber is very rare on Crete even around 1300 BC when it is otherwise widely known in Greece, though in smaller quantities than before. Ironically, this the period of richly furnished graves in Denmark, with very many metal artefacts and complete woollen garments. Some intricate amber beads from Greece have parallels as far away as southern Britain (gold-capped and spacers), Central Europe and Denmark (spacers) (Bouzek 1966, 267 Fig. 24). Strangely, Baltic amber is uncommon in the Balkans in this period and likely reached the Aegean by way of the Adriatic. Other objects demonstrate Aegean links with the Balkans and eastern Central Europe as well as beyond in the same period (e.g. Bouzek 1966; Randsborg 1967; Lomborg 1967; Vladár 1973; Schauer 1985; Sherratt 1997, e.g. 421ff.; etc.).

Amber and other artefacts and features may delineate routes of contact and exchange, common aristocratic lifestyles, religious beliefs and joint cultic interest, but these alone cannot account for the spread of metals far beyond the mining areas in truly impressive quantities, not least towards the North. Significantly, East Prussia and Lithuania, with enormous deposits of amber, are rather poor in bronzes in the Early Bronze Age (Sidrys & Luchtanas 1999). At the close of the Bronze Age in the North this amber streamed southward to play a major role in, for instance, Northern Italy. By then, a modern Mediterranean economy was demanding raw materials in large quantities from Europe; consequently bronze almost disappeared from Denmark, which launched its own production of iron, indeed an Iron Age.

Textiles are the most likely means of exchange in the Bronze Age proper. Only textiles offer labour-intensive goods which can be widely produced and distributed, talents and organisation permitting, and which seem to carry high prices for exactly these reasons. The wrap in the Skrydstrup grave would have provided enough bronze in contemporary Hittite Anatolia for 100 Nordic bronze swords (but possibly fewer in the Aegean). Such differences in value would spur on exchange even over considerable distances and through various intermediaries.

That the system of exchange was not a simple one is probably revealed by the differences in technical character and even in quality between textiles from Denmark and Thüringen (Thuringia) in Central Europe, the latter being somewhat finer and with a different combination of spinning directions for the treads (Table 16). Such elegant textiles would have been valued in many social environments. In addition, wools differ (with the sheep) which encourages selective breeding, and also exchange. Such archaeological patterns should reflect specialisation and improvement in quality – a prerequisite for a further rise in demand. Diocletian's Edict has particularly high prices for woollen cloaks and other such garments from the European areas of the Late Roman Empire beyond the Mediterranean, for instance Gaul and upper Danubian provinces, no doubt reflecting dramatic differences in quality of wools and finished products (Frank 1940/V, 369f./E.R. Graser).

It should be clear that exchange in amber, ordinary trade in metals, common aristocratic cultural and social norms, and even commonly held beliefs and joint cultic events, do not suffice to explain the surprising distribution of gold and bronze across large parts of Europe beyond the Mediterranean in the Bronze Age. But the production and distribution of textiles could. Fine textiles, being relatively cheap in raw materials but highly labour-intensive, are exactly what 'peripheries' are capable of providing for the 'centres'.

Around 2000 BC palaces were erected on Crete, and a little later on the Greek mainland. At the same time, the Balkans, Central and even Western Europe, as well as the North, see a marked development in metallurgy, not least in the number of metal artefacts produced. This is the period when we expect – indeed, can demonstrate – that the textile industry and exchange in Central Europe and the North was taking off, along with mining and other crafts, thus *producing* the Bronze Age.

5. Europe and Beyond

In conclusion, basic economics account for Bronze Age exchanges, motivated by cultural requests, since subsistence was largely satisfied locally.

6

Conclusions

... only the dead have real power.

Bassari informant, Togo

The cloth types of the Nordic Early Bronze Age were all simple tabbies but seemingly woven to certain particular sizes. Pattern and sewing skills are high, fulling (stamping) is common, and there were embroideries and fine belts, among other time-consuming details. The industry was probably highly organised, all the way from sheep ranching to production of the largest textiles.

In contrast to the female ones, male garments have not aroused much functional discussion: loincloth or coat, cloak and caps – a heavy one for fighting and a pixie-cap for daily use, even at night. Male garments are well defined, in fact rather restricted, as to function and fashion. Leather sandals and foot-wrappings for 'socks', the latter also used by women, complete the common outfit, even though we may surmise that hide or fur coats were also applied against the cold. A male cult garment consists of a T-shirt open to the sides with two V-shaped tongues serving as a breechcloth.

Women's clothing in the Early and even in the Late Bronze Age comprised a blouse or T-shirt covering the upper part of the body. A short string skirt – such as the one in the famous Egtved grave of a young woman – was no doubt used by younger members of cult groups (cf. figurines in acrobatic poses), whether unmarried or married, but would also have functioned as a skirt for the warmer half of the year, as indicated by many summer burials of women in string skirts. A long plain skirt was also worn (Fig. 18, cf. Fig. 20). A similar piece of cloth might have been used for carrying babies (on the back, in African fashion). A very large and thick wrap – the traditional 'heavy skirt' – would have served to shroud the whole body, for instance on special occasions, like ceremonies; it may have doubled as a bedsheet-cum-cover.

Certainly, the wraps from the graves of Skrydstrup and Borum Eshøj cannot be conceived of as 'skirts', as most archaeologists claim (cf. Fig. 14). In these graves, crudely tacked belted wraps were wound around the lower bodies of the women, and since no other skirts were found (or rather identified), it was believed that the toga-sized wraps were in fact skirts. Very large 'blankets' from female graves could also function as wraps (cf. Fig. 18); folded, they might even have served as double skirts. The smaller blankets from male graves were likely bedsheets, the cloak doubling as cover. In comparison with male dress, female garments are less restricted as to function and fashion. They are also more conspicuous, as is female jewellery.

Hair was worn short by young women, longer by both young and old women, and if so in elaborate coiffures. In the grave, women were accompanied by various artefacts in gold and bronze, including necklaces (and neck collars), belt-plates – images of the sun – tutuli (small suns, or rather 'stars'), and daggers. It is suggested that the daggers link certain women by marriage to male 'sword bearers'. Male bossed upper class tutuli in the female Ølby grave (Fig. 4), for instance, point in the same direction, as does the broken tip of a sword's blade in the same grave, substituting for a dagger. Necklaces (and neck collars) indicate married status, while belt-plates (images of the sun) indicate a role in cultic performances; the same is the case with belt-boxes (Period III), containers for amulets: in the Late Bronze Age these become very large and very conspicuous female status symbols.

While men may have more bronze and gold as grave goods than women, in particular weapons, mainly swords, and artefacts pertaining to social status and role, including imported artefacts, the women had more textiles, plus items related to ritual functions and cosmology (Figs 12-13; Table 10). Since textiles were probably very costly, the greater amount of female garments probably balanced the relations between genders more than the metal artefacts alone would indicate. Most of the bronzes in female graves are jewellery, and very few items are imported. On the whole, the equipment of women reflects local or regional society rather than foreign connections. The statuses of women are summarised in Table 14, mainly using artefact criteria. Outline suggestions regarding rank and statuses of men follow in Table 15, using the same method (cf. Randsborg & Christensen 2006).

Solving riddles of composite female dress is but one step towards understanding the biographies and values of the elites of the Nordic Bronze Age with the help of textiles and grave goods. Male dress is seemingly easier to comprehend, as are most of the male grave goods, such as the weapons, particular badges (bossed tutuli), folding stools, and steering sticks for chariot horses. The male gold bracelets and other golden items are clearly tokens of high rank. Among the minor items, the function of razors is evident, but the tweezers are still a puzzle – for the toilet, or a surgical instrument? Only men carry flint strike-a-lights, indication of their range as compared to the females: the latter travelling with men, or staying 'at home'. Drinking vessels for symposiae, like foreign artefacts, are not uncommon among the men, who were evidently in charge of 'diplomacy' and foreign contact and, in particular, the acquisition of metals (all are imported into the North) and certain sorts of knowledge.

It is surmised that a long knotted string with tufts of cattle-tail hair found in a small box placed at the head of the young woman in the Egtved grave, along with liquid-absorbing mosses and a wad of fine lambswool is part of a 'sanitary belt' (Fig. 28; cf. Table 9). The napkin of the belt may actually have been used to wrap the cremated bones of a smaller child at the foot end of the coffin, likely a sacrifice, since the child cannot have been the dead woman's own. A similar arrangement, in fact, a napkin to go with a plain belt, is found in the same position in the Skrydstrup grave of a young woman; a third one in the Borum Eshøj grave (old lady), also to go with a plain, non-decorative belt (decorative belts with large tassels are present in both the Egtved and the Borum Eshøj grave). In the latter case the napkin is thick and may have served other hygienic functions.

Nakedness is found with deities and their companions and followers, and may well have been a significant element in cult performances (Figs 23f.; cf. Tables 11-12). Semi-nakedness is reminiscent of West African respect shown towards high-ranking persons, and towards spirits and deities at sacred localities by baring the upper body. Small standing female figurines, naked but for a necklace and perhaps a few other items, are possibly fertility goddesses (the vagina is stressed). Semi-naked active figurines are parts of larger representations (there are tenons under the feet of the beings), likely involving deities and their companions, possibly even initiated followers. Similar images occur on razors and may appear on rock-carvings too.

Despite the local character of female jewellery, main elements of female dress, like the blouse or T-shirt and the long plain skirt, occur both in the North and further south in Europe. Even the string skirt seems to have parallels in Central Europe. A version of the short-sleeved blouse occurs in the Aegean, where the long skirt is sometimes voluminous with horizontal pleats. The large wrap is probably common everywhere. The only Nordic female garment that seems to be unknown in the Aegean Bronze Age is the ancient string skirt. Yet Homer may have dreamt about it when describing Hera's seduction of Zeus,

> ... then sashed her waist with a waistband
> floating a hundred tassels, ...
>
> *Iliad* XIV.221

This is evidence for a European female *koinê* in dress, parallel, no doubt, to a male one. Male loincloths and cloaks are found in the Aegean; a fur cloak is known from a Dutch bog body (Fig. 29); in the early first millennium BC, Italian cloaks have the same kidney-shape that we encounter in Jylland (Jutland) some five hundred years earlier and with Roman soldiers half a millennium later. Such similarities in dress across very large distances would have encouraged exchange in textiles.

From around 2000 BC palaces were erected in the Aegean. At the same time, the Balkans, Central and Western Europe, and even the North see a marked development in metallurgy, not least in the number of manufactured metal artefacts. This is also the period in which we expect the textile industry and exchange of wool and cloth to be taking off in Central Europe and the North, thus *producing* the Bronze Age. In other words, basic economics accounts for Bronze Age production and exchange, motivated by social, cultural and religious requirements.

Prices of textiles were very high in the East Mediterranean civilisations in the Bronze Age, indicating that trade in wool, cloth and certainly in garments were lucrative businesses based on female work (Tables 17-18). It is imagined that this was the case across the whole spectrum of Prehistoric Europe. Even though Denmark may not have exported textiles to Babylon, the Skrydstrup wrap alone would have bought enough bronze in Hittite Anatolia to produce one hundred sword blades in Jylland, while a hundred sword blades in Jylland, one is inclined to believe, could have bought a parish or a couple of magnificent boats.

If this model is accepted, it will explain, for instance, the huge amounts of bronze and gold in the Northern Bronze Age; a phenomenon that the amber trade was never able to explain. It will also explain why certain areas with no sheep, or only few, have few bronzes. To balance the proposition, we should not forget regional differences in cloth, technologically as well as in terms of quality (cf. Tables 2; 16-17). Such observations argue against massive trade, at least over very long distances.

Finally, looking towards the future, stable isotope and DNA

studies will no doubt be applied to the unique Bronze Age material, delineating patterns of transportation of wool and exchange of garments. Even more important is the collection of more data across Europe and beyond. Most important is to test the theory of the crucial importance of local production and supra-regional exchange of woollen textiles in the European and Near Eastern Bronze Age. Textiles as a major cultural factor have been overlooked by both older and more recent surveys of the Bronze Age. Exciting analyses, discussions and scientific debates are to come.

Bibliography

Aagaard, K. 1802. Physisk, oeconomisk og topografisk Beskrivelse over Thye beliggende i Thisted Amt, Aalborg Stift. Et Forsøg. Viborg (Fønss).

AK = Aner & Kersten 1973ff.

Alexandersen, V., P. Bennike, L. Hvass & K.-H. Stærmose Nielsen. 1981. Egtved-pigen: nye undersøgelser. Aarbøger for Nordisk Old-kyndighed og Historie 1981. 17ff.

Alram-Stern, E. & G. Nightingale (eds). 2007. Keimelion. Eliten-buildung und elitärer Konsum von der mykenischen Palastzeit bis zur homerischen Epoche. /The Formation of Elites and elitist Life-styles from Mycenean Palatial Times to the Homeric Period. Akten des internationalen Kongresses vom 3. Bis 5. Februar 2005 in Salzburg. Österreichichische Akademie der Wissen-schaften. Philosophisch-historische Klasse. Denkschriften 350. Veröffentlichungen der mykenischen Kommission 27. Wien (Öster-reichichische Akademie der Wissenschaften).

Althin, C.-A. 1945. Studien zu den bronzezeitlichen Felszeichnungen von Skåne I-II. Lund (Gleerup).

Aner, E. & K. Kersten (& K.-H. Willroth, for later volumes, with E. Koch) (eds). 1973ff. Dic Funde der älteren Bronzezeit des Nordis-chen Kreises in Dänemark, Schleswig-Holstein und Niedersachsen. Iff. København (Nationalmuseet) & Neumünster (Wachholz).

Barber, E.J.W. 1991. Prehistoric Textiles. The Development of Cloth in the Neolithic and Bronze Ages. With Special Reference to the Aegean. Princeton (Princeton University Press).

Barker, G. & C. Gamble (eds). 1985. Beyond Domestication in Prehis-toric Europe. Investigations in Subsistence Archaeology and Social Complexity. London (Academic Press).

Baudou, E. 1960. Die regionale und chronologische Einteilung der jüngeren Bronzezeit im Nordischen Kreis. Acta Universitatis

Bibliography

Stockholmiensis. Studies in North-European Archaeology 1. Stockholm (Almqvist & Wiksell).

Becker, C., M.-L. Dunkelmann, C. Metzner-Nebelsick, H. Peter-Röcher, M. Roeder & B. Teržan (eds). 1997. Χρόνος. Beiträge zur prähistorischen Archäologie zwischen Nord- und Südosteuropa. Festschrift für Bernhard Hänsel. Internationale Archäologie. Studia honoraria 1. Espelkamp (Marie Leidorf).

Bender Jørgensen, L. 1986. Forhistoriske textiler i Skandinavien. Nordiske Fortidsminder. Series B. Vol. 9. København (Kongelige nordiske Oldskriftselskab).

———. 1992. North European Textiles until AD 1000. Aarhus (Aarhus University Press).

Bender Jørgensen, L., E. Munksgaard & K.-H. Stærmose Nielsen. 1982. Melhøj-fundet. En hidtil upåagtet parallel til Skrydstrupfundet. Aarbøger for Nordisk Oldkyndighed og Historie 1982. 19ff.

Bender Jørgensen, L. & E. Munksgaard. 1992. Archaeological Textiles in Northern Europe. Report from the 4th NESAT Symposium 1-5 May 1990 in Copenhagen. Tidens Tand 5. København (Konservatorskolen. Det Kongelige Danske Kunstakademi).

van den Berghe, I., M. Gleba & U. Mannering. 2009. Towards the Identification of Dyestuffs from Early Iron Age Scandinavian Peat Bog Textiles. Journal of Archaeological Science 36. 1910ff.

Birket-Smith, K. 1937. Vævede Kapper fra Nordvest-Indianerne. Fra Nationalmuseets Arbejdsmark 1937. 49ff.

Blier, S.P. 1998. The Royal Arts of Africa. The Majesty of Form. New York & London (Abrams & Laurence King).

Boas, N.A. 1983. Egehøj. A Settlement from the Early Bronze Age in East Jutland. Journal of Danish Archaeology 2. 90ff.

Boe, K.M., T. Capelle & C. Fischer (eds). 2009. Tollundmandens verden. Kontinentale kontakter i tidlig jernalder. Højbjerg/Silkeborg (Wormianum/Silkeborg Kulturhistoriske Museum).

Bouzek, J. 1966. The Aegean and Central Europe. An Introduction to the Study of Cultural Interrelations 1600-1300 BC. Památky Archeologické LVII:1. 242ff.

Boye = Boye 1896.

Boye, V. 1896. Fund af Egekister fra Bronzealderen i Danmark. Et monografisk Bidrag til Belysning af Bronzealderens Kultur. Kjøbenhavn (Høst). [Reprinted by Wormianum 1986.]

Breuning-Madsen, H. & M. Holst. 1992-93. Genesis of Iron Pans in Bronze Age Mounds in Denmark. Journal of Danish Archaeology 11. 80ff.

Bibliography

Briard, J. 1965. Les dépôts bretons et l'âge du bronze atlantique. Rennes (Becdelièvre).

Broholm, H.C. 1943-49. Danmarks Bronzealder I-IV. København (Nyt Nordisk/Arnold Busck).

Broholm, H.C. & M. Hald. 1929-35. Danske Bronzealders Dragter. Nordiske Fortidsminder II. 215ff. København (Det kgl. Nordiske Oldskriftselskab/Gyldendal).

——— (et al.). 1939. Skrydstrupfundet. Nordiske Fortidsminder III:2. København (Det kgl. Nordiske Oldskriftselskab/Gyldendal).

———. 1940. Costumes of the Bronze Age in Denmark. Contributions to the Archaeology and Textile-History of the Bronze Age. Copenhagen (Nyt Nordisk/Busck). [Cf. Broholm & Hald 1929-35; 1939.]

Broholm, H.C., W.P. Larsen & G. Skjerne. 1949. The Lures of the Bronze Age. Copenhagen (Gyldendal).

Brøndsted, J. 1934. Inedita aus dem dänischen Nationalmuseeum I. Acta Archaeologica V. 145ff.

Brongers, J.A. & P.J. Woltering. 1973. Prehistory in the Netherlands: An Economic-Technological Approach. Berichten van de Rijksdienst voor het Oudheidkundig Bodemonderzoek (BROB) 23. 7ff.

Bryce, T. 1998. The Kingdom of the Hittites. Oxford (Oxford University Press).

———. 2002. Life and Society in the Hittite World. Oxford (Oxford University Press).

Burenhult, G. 1973. The Rock Carvings of Götaland (excluding Gothenburg county, Bohuslän and Dalsland) Part II: Illustrations. Acta Archaeologica Lundensia. Series in 4°. N° 8. Lund/Bonn (Gleerup/Habelt).

———. 1980. Götalands hällristningar I (utom Göteborgs och Bohus län samt Dalsland)/The Rock-Carvings of Götaland I (excluding Gothenburg county, Bohuslän and Dalsland). Thesis and Papers in North-European Archaeology 10. [Stockholm] (Burenhult).

Burney, C. 2004. Historical Dictionary of the Hittites. Historical Dictionaries of Ancient Civilizations and Historical Eras 14. Lanham (Scarecrow).

Carapanos, C. 1878. Dodone et ses ruines. Texte & Plaches. Paris (Hachette).

von Carnap-Bornheim, C. & C. Radtke (eds). 2007. Es war einmal ein Schiff. Archäologische Expeditionen zum Meer. Hamburg (mare).

Clark, P. (ed.). 2009. Bronze Age Connections. Cultural Contact in Prehistoric Europe. Oxford (Oxbow).

Coffyn, A., J. Gomez & J.P. Mohen. 1981. L'apogée du bronze atlantique. Le dépôt de Vénat. L'âge de Bronze en France 1. Paris (Picard).

Coles, J. 2005. Shadows of a Northern Past. Rock Carvings of Bohuslän and Østfold. Oxford (Oxbow Books).

Davidsen, K. 1982. Journal of Danish Archaeology 1. Bronze Age Houses at Jegstrup, near Skive, Central Jutland. 65ff.

DB = Broholm 1943-49/Vol. If.

Dierck, A. 1976. Tatauierung in der vor- und frühgeschichtlicher Zeit. Archäologisches Korrespondenzblatt 6. 169ff.

Djupedal, R. & H.C. Broholm. 1952. Marcus Schnabel og bronzealderfundet fra Grevensvænge. Aarbøger for Nordisk Oldkyndighed og Historie 1952. 5ff.

Drack, W. (ed.). 1969. Ur- und frühgeschichtliche Archäologie der Schweiz II. Die Jüngere Steinzeit. Basel (Schweizerische Gesellschaft für Ur- und Frühgeschichte).

Dumitrescu, V. 1961. Necropola de incinerație din epoca bronzului de la Cîrna. Biblioteca de Arheologie IV. București (Institutul de Arheologie al Academiei R.P.R.).

Ebbesen, K. 1995a. Spätneolitische Schmuckmode. Acta Archaeologica 66. 219ff.

———. 1995b. Die nordischen Bernsteinhorte der Trichterbecherkultur. Praehistorische Zeitschrift 70:1. 32ff.

Edwards, C. 1904/1971. The Hammurabi Code and the Sinaitic Legislation. With a Complete Translation of the Great Babylonian Inscription Discovered at Susa. Port Washington/London (Kennikat).

Egevang, R., C. Ejlers, B. Friis, O. Højrup & E. Munksgaard (eds). 1981. Det skabende menneske 1-2. Kulturhistoriske skitser tilegnet P.V. Glob 20. februar 1981. København (Nationalmuseet).

Egg, M. (et al.). 1996. Das hallstattzeitliche Fürstengrab von Strettweg bei Judenburg in der Obersteiermark. Römisch-Germanisches Zentralmuseum Monographien 37. Bonn (Habelt).

Egg, M. & K. Spindler (etc.). 2009. Kleidung und Ausrüstung der kupferzeitlichen Gletschermumie aus den Ötztaler Alpen. Monographien des Römisch-Germanischen Zentralmuseums 77. Der Mann im Eis 6. Mainz (RGZM).

Elis, P. von (ed.). 2002. Guerriero e sacerdote. Autorià e comunità nell'età del ferro a Verucchio. La Tomba del Trono. Quaderni di archeologia dell'Emilia Romagna 6. Firenze (del Giglio).

Engelhardt, C. 1871. Romerske Statuetter og andre Kunstgjenstande fra den tidlige nordiske Jernalder. Aarbøger for Nordisk Oldkyndighed og Historie 1871. 432ff.

Bibliography

Eskildsen, L. & E. Lomborg. 1976. Giftetanker. Skalk 1976:5. 18ff.

————. 1977. Skørtejægere. Skalk 1977:4. 3ff.

Farke, H. 1993. Textile Reste von Dietzhausen und Schwarza. Alt-Thüringen 27. 109ff.

Feustel, R. 1958. Bronzezeitliche Hügelgräberkultur im Gebiet von Schwarza (Südthüringen). Veröffentlichungen des Museums für Ur- und Frühgeschichte Thüringens I. Weimar (Böhlau).

Frank, T. (ed.). 1940. Rome and Italy of the Empire. An Economic Survey of Ancient Rome V. Baltimore (Johns Hopkins University Press). [Later reprints.]

Frei, K.M., R. Frei, U. Mannering, M. Gleba, M.L. Nosch & H. Lyngstrøm. 2009. Provenance of ancient Textiles – a Pilot Study Evaluating the Strontium Isotope System in Wool. Archaeometry 51:2. 252ff.

Frei, K.M., I. Skals, M. Gleba & H. Lyngstrøm. 2009. The Huldremose Iron Age Textiles, Denmark. An Attempt to Define their Provenance Applying the Strontium Isotope System. Journal of Archaeological Science 36. 1965ff.

Frey, O.H. 1969. Die Entstehung der Situlenkunst. Studien zur figürlich verzierten Toreutik von Este. Römisch-germanische Forschungen 31. Berlin (de Gruyter).

Gimbutas, M. 1982. The Goddesses and Gods of Old Europe 6500-3500 BC. Myths and Cult Images. London (Thames & Hudson). 2nd edn.

Gleba, M. 2008. Textile Production in Pre-Roman Italy. Ancient Textiles Series 4. Oxford (Oxbow Books).

Glob, P.V. 1944. Studier over den jyske Enkeltgravskultur. Aarbøger for Nordisk Oldkyndighed og Historie 1944. 1ff.

————. 1952. Danske Oldsager II. Yngre Stenalder. Udgivet af Nationalmuseets Embedsmænd. Under Redaktion af Therkel Mathiassen. København (Gyldendal).

————. 1969. Hellristninger i Danmark. Jysk Arkæologisk Selskabs Skrifter VII. Højbjerg/København (Jysk Arkæologisk Selskab/Gyldendal).

Goldhahn, J. (ed.). 2005. Mellan sten och järn I-II. Rapport från det 9:e nordiska bronsålderssymposiet, Göteborg 2003-10-09/12. Gotarc Serie C. Arkeologiska Skrifter 59.

Grömer, K. 2006. Textilien der Bronzezeit in Mitteleuropa. Archaeologia Austriaca 90. 31ff.

————. 2007. Bronzezeitliche Gewebefunde aus Hallstatt. Ihr Kontext in der Textilkunde Mitteleuropas und die Entwicklung der Textiltechnologie zur Eisenzeit. Wien (Universität Wien, Ur- und Frühgeschichte). (Unpublished PhD thesis.)

Hald, M. 1930. Brikvævning i danske Oldtidsfund. Aarbøger for Nordisk Oldkyndighed og Historie 1930. 277ff.

———. 1950. Olddanske Tekstiler. Komparative tekstil- og dragthistoriske Studier paa Grundlag af Mosefund og Gravfund fra Jernalderen. Nordiske Fortidsminder 5. København (Det Kongelige Nordiske Oldskriftselskab).

———. 1980. Ancient Danish Textiles from Bogs and Burials. A Comparative Study of Costume and Iron Age Textiles. Publications of the National Museum. Archaeological-Historical Series XXI. Copenhagen (National Museum). [Danish edition 1950, cf. above.]

———. 1972 Primitive Shoes. An Archaeological-Ethnological Study Based upon Shoe Finds from the Jutland Peninsula. Publications of the National Museum. Archaeological-Historical Series I:XIII. Copenhagen (National Museum).

Hansen, S. 2007. Bilder vom Menschen der Steinzeit. Untersuchungen zur anthropomorphen Plastik der Jungsteinzeit und Kupferzeit in Südosteuropa I-II. Archäologie in Eurasien 20. Mainz (Deutsches Archäologisches Institut. Eurasien-Abteilung/von Zabern).

Harald Hansen, H. 1978. Skrydstrup-kvindens dragt. Aarbøger for Nordisk Oldkyndighed og Historie 1978. 139ff.

Harding, A.F. 2000. European Societies in the Bronze Age. Cambridge (Cambridge University Press).

Harding, A. & H. Hughes-Brock (etc.). 1974. Amber in the Mycenaean World. The Annual of the British School of Athens 69. 145ff.

Heltzer, M. 1978. Goods, Prices and the Organization of Trade in Ugarit. Marketing and Transportation in the Eastern Mediterranean in the Second Half of the II Millennium BCE. Wiesbaden (Reichert).

Herrmann, J. (ed.). 1989. Archäologie in der Deutschen Demokratischen Republik. Denkmale und Funde 1. Archäologische Kulturen, geschichtliche Perioden und Volksstämme. Stuttgart (Theiss).

Herskovits, M.J. 1938. Dahomey. An Ancient West African Kingdom I-II. New York (Augustin).

Hoffner, H.A., Jr. 1997. The Laws of the Hittites. A Critical Edition. Documenta et Monumenta Orientis Antiqui 23. Leiden (Brill).

Höpfel, F., W. Platzer & K. Spindler (eds). 1992. Der Mann im Eis 1. Bericht über das Internationale Symposium 1992 in Innsbruck.

Bibliography

Veröffentlichungen der Universität Innsbruck 187. Innsbruck (Universität Innsbruck).

Horst, F. 1985. Zedau. Eine jungbronze- und eisenzeitliche Siedlung in der Altmark. Schriften zur Ur- und Frühgeschichte 36. Berlin (Akademie-Verlag).

Hvass, L. 1981. Egtvedpigen. København (Sesam).

Janssen, J.J. 1975. Commodity Prices from the Ramessid Period. An Economic Study of the Village of Necropolis Workmen at Thebes. Leiden (Brill).

Jenkins, D. (ed.). 2002. The Cambridge History of Western Textiles I-II. New York (Cambridge University Press).

Jensen, J. 1979. Danmarkshistorien. Bronzealderen 1-2. Skovlandets folk & Guder og mennesker. København (sesam).

———. 1998. Manden i kisten. Hvad bronzealderens gravhøje gemte. København (Gyldendal).

Jochenhövel, A. 1971. Die Rasiermesser in Mitteleuropa. Prähistorische Bronzefunde VIII:1. München (Beck).

———. 1991. Räumliche Mobilität von Personen in der mitteren Bronzezeit des westlichen Mitteleuropa. Germania 69. 49ff.

Jochenhövel, A. & W. Kubach. 1994. Bronzezeit in Deutschland. Stuttgart (Theiss).

Jöns, H. & F. Lüth (eds). 2004. Mythos und Magie. Archäologische Schätze der Bronzezeit aus Mecklenburg-Vorpommern. Archäologie in Mecklenburg-Vorpommern 3. Lübstorf (Archäologisches Landesmuseum & Landesamt für Bodendenkmalpflege Mecklenburg-Vorpommern).

Jöris, O. 2008. Der altpaläolitische Fundplatz Dmanisi (Georgien, Kaukasus). Archäologische Funde und Befunde des liegenden Fundkomplexes im Kontext der frühen Menschheitsentwicklung. Monographien des Römisch-Germanischen Zentralmuseums 74. Mainz (Römisch-Germanisches Zentralmuseum).

Just, F. 1964. Vor- und frügeschichtliche Gewerbereste aus Mecklenburg. Bodendenkmalpflege in Mecklenburg 1964. 303ff.

Karlsson, S. 2005. Kroppens gestaltning och symbolik på Sydskandinaviens hällristningar. Goldhahn 2005/II. 461ff.

Kastelic, J. 1965. Situla Art. Ceremonial Bronzes of Ancient Europe. London (Thames & Hudson).

Kaul, F. 1991. En dansk ældre bronzealders kultøkse fra Meuse i Belgien. Aarbøger for Nordisk Oldkyndighed og Historie 1991. 59ff.

———. 1998. Ships on Bronzes. A Study in Bronze Age Religion and Iconography I-II. PNM - Publications from the National Museum.

127

Bibliography

Studies in Archaeology & History 3:1-2. Copenhagen (National Museum).

———. 2004. Bronzealderens religion. Studier af den nordiske bronzealders ikonografi. Nordiske Fortidsminder. Serie B 22. København (Det kgl. Nordiske Oldskriftselskab/Lynge).

Kaul, F. & M. Freudenberg. 2007. Sonne und Schiff. Die Schiffsdarstellungen des Nordens in der Bronzezeit. von Carnap-Bornheim & Radtke 2007. 77ff.

Kaul, F. & K. Randsborg. 2008. Hurtige vogne. Skalk 2008:2. 3ff.

Kersten K. [1936.] Zur älteren nordischen Bronzezeit. Veröffentlichungen der Schleswig-Holsteinischen Universitätsgesellschaft II:3. Neumünster (Wachholtz).

Køie, M. 1943. Tøj fra yngre Bronzealder fremstillet af nælde (*Urtica dioeca L.*). Aarbøger for Nordisk Oldkyndighed og Historie 1943. 99ff.

Kosmowska-Ceranowicz, B. & H. Paner 1999. Investigations into amber. Proceedings of the International Interdisciplinary Symposium: Baltic Amber and Other Fossil Resins. 997 Urbs Gyddanyzc – 1997 Gdansk. 2-6 September 1997, Gdansk. Gdansk (The Archaeological museum in Gdansk. Museum of the Earth, Polish Academy of Sciences).

Kristiansen, K. 1974. Glerupfundet. Et depotfund med kvindesmykker fra bronzealderens femte periode. Hikuin 1. 7ff.

Kristiansen, K. & T.B. Larsson. 2005. The Rise of Bronze Age Society. Travels, Transmissions and Transformations. Cambridge (Cambridge University Press).

Larsson, L. 1973-74. The Fogdarp find. A hoard from the Late Bronze Age. Meddelanden från Lunds universitets historiska museum 1973-74. 169ff.

Laux, F. 1981-83. Flügelhauben und andere Kopfbedeckungen der bronzezeitlichen Lüneburger Gruppe. Hammaburg NF 6. 49ff.

Linge, T.E. 2005. Kammeranlegget i Mjeltehaugen – eit rekonstruksjonsforslag. Goldhahn 2005/II. 537ff.

Lipiński, E. 2000. The Aramaeans. Their Ancient History, Culture, Religion. Orientalia Lovaniensia Analecta 100. Leeuven (Peeters/Departement Oosterse Studies).

Liversage, D. 2000. Interpreting Impurity Patterns in Ancient Bronze: Denmark. Nordiske Fortidsminder. Serie C:1. København (Det kongelige nordiske Oldskriftselskab).

Lomborg, E. 1963. Skrydstrup-frisure fra en brandgrav på Mors. Aarbøger for Nordisk Oldkyndighed og Historie 1963. 31ff.

———. 1964. Hvilshøjkvindens hår. Skalk 1964:2. 10ff.

Bibliography

————. 1967. An Amber Spacer-bead from Denmark. Antiquity XLI No. 163. 221ff.

————. 1975. Tidlig ten. Skalk 1975:1. 15.

————. 1981. Et tøjstykke fra Hvidegårdsfundet. Egevang et al. 1981. 64ff.

Madsen, A.P. 1868. Afbildninger af Danske Oldsager og Mindesmærker. Steenalderen. Kjøbenhavn (Rasmussen).

Malmer, M.P. 1992. Weight Systems in the Scandinavian Bronze Age. Antiquity 66 (No. 251). 377ff.

Mannering, U. 2009. Dragten i tidlig jernalder. Boe et al. 2009. 98ff.

Mannering, U., M. Gleba, G. Possnert & J. Heinemeier. 2009. Om datering af mosefundne lig og beklædningsdele. Kuml 2009. 103ff.

Manning, S.W., C.B. Ramsey, W. Kutschera, T. Higham, B. Kromer, P. Steier, E.M. Wild. 2006. Chronology for the Aegean Late Bronze Age 1700-1400 B.C. Science 312; No. 5773. 565ff.

Margalit, B. 1981. The Geographical Setting of the Aqht Story. Young 1981. 131ff.

————. 1989. The Ugaritic Poem of AQHT. Text, Translation, Commentary. Beihefte zur Zeitschrift für die alttestamentliche Wissenschaft 182. Berlin (de Gruyter).

Marinatos, S. (& M. Hirmer). 1960. Crete and Mycenae. London (Thames & Hudson).

Marková, K. 1999. Bernsteinfunde im Karpatenbacken. Kosmowska-Ceranowicz & Paner 1999. 111ff.

McDowell, A.G. 1999. Village Life in Ancient Egypt. Laundry Lists and Love Songs. Oxford (Oxford University Press).

Mederos, A. & C.C. Lamberg-Karlovsky. 2001. Converting Currencies in the Old World. Nature 411. 437ff.

Meissner. B. 1936. Warenpreise in Babylonien. Abhandlungen der preussischen Akademie der Wissenschaften. Philosophisch-historische Klasse 1936:1. Berlin (Akademie der Wissenschaften). 1ff.

Merkyte, I. (et al.). 2005. Lîga. Copper Age Strategies in Bulgaria. Acta Archaeologica 76:1. Acta Archaeologica Supplementa VI. Centre of World Archaeology (CWA) Publications 2. København (Blackwell Munksgaard).

Milstreu, G. & H. Prøhl (eds.). 1996. Dokumentation och registrering av hällristningar i Tanum 1. Aspeberget. Tanumshede (Tanum Hällristningsmuseum Underslös).

————. 1999. Dokumentation och registrering av hällristningar i Tanum 2. Fossum med angränsande områden. Tanumshede (Tanum Hällristningsmuseum Underslös).

129

Bibliography

Müller, S. 1920. Billed- og Fremstillingskunst i Bronzealderen. Aarbøger for Nordisk Oldkyndighed og Historie 1920. 125ff.

———. 1921. Bronzealderens Kunst i Danmark. Kjøbenhavn (Reitzel).

Müller-Karpe, H. 1980. Handbuch der Vorgeschichte IV:1-3. Bronzezeit. München (Beck).

Munksgaard, E. 1974. Oldtidsdragter. København (Nationalmuseet).

Naue, J. 1894. Die Bronzezeit in Oberbayern. Ergebnisse der Ausgrabungen und Untersuchungen von Hügelgräbern der Bronzezeit zwischen Ammer- und Staffelsee und in der Nähe des Starnbergersees. I-II (Album). München (Piloty & Löhle).

Nielsen, K.-H. 1971. Tilskæring. Skalk 1971:5. 13ff.

Niwinski, A. 1999. Amber in Ancient Egypt. Kosmowska-Ceranowicz & Paner 1999. 115ff.

Norling-Christensen, H. 1943. Bronzealderhjælmene fra Viksø. Fra Nationalmuseets Arbejdsmark 1943. 5ff.

Novotná, M. 1980. Die Nadeln in der Slowakei. Prähistorische Bronzefunde XIII:6. München (Beck).

Oldeberg, A.1974. Die ältere Metallzeit in Schweden I. Stockholm (Kungl. Vitterhets Historie och Antikvitets Akademien).

Piesker, H. 1958. Untersuchungen zur älteren lüneburgischen Bronzezeit. Lüneburg (Nordwestdeutsche Verband für Altertumsforschung & Urgeschichtliche Sammlung Landesmuseum Hannover).

Poulsen, J. (ed.). 1989. Regionale forhold i nordisk bronzealder. 5. Nordiske Symposium for Bronzealderforskning på Sandbjerg Slot 1987. Jysk arkæologisk Selskabs Skrifter 24. Højbjerg (Jysk Arkæologisk Selskab).

Probst, E. (ed.). 1996. Deutschland in der Bronzezeit. Bauern, Bronzegiesser und Burgherren zwischen Nordsee und Alpen. München (Bertelsmann).

Randsborg, K. 1967. 'Aegean' Bronzes in a Grave in Jutland. Acta Archaeologica XXXVIII, 1ff.

———. 1968. Von Periode II zu III. Chronologische Studien über die ältere Bronzezeit Südskandinaviens und Norddeutschlands. Acta Archaeologica XXXIX. 1ff.

———. 1980. The Viking Age in Denmark. The Formation of a State. London (Duckworth) & New York (St Martin's).

———. 1984. A Bronze Age Grave on Funen Containing a Metal Worker's Tools. Acta Archaeologica 55. 185ff.

———. 1985. Subsistence and Settlement in Northern Temperate Europe in the First Millennium A.D. Barker & Gamble 1985. 233ff.

Bibliography

————. 1993. Kivik. Archaeology & Iconography. Acta Archaeologica 64:1.

————. 2010. Bronze Age Chariots. From Wheel & Yoke to Goad & Double-arm Knob. Acta Archaeologica 81. 251ff.

Randsborg, K. & K. Christensen. 2006. Bronze Age Oak-Coffin Graves. Archaeology & Dendro-Dating. Acta Archaeologica 77. Acta Archaeologica Supplementa VII. Centre of World Archaeology (CWA) – Publications 3.

Randsborg, K. & C. Nybo. 1984. The Coffin & the Sun. Demography and Ideology in Scandinavian Prehistory. Acta Archaeologica 55. 161ff.

Rieck, F.R. 1971-72. Bronzer fra Vognserup Enge. Fra Holbæk Amt. Årbog for Historisk Samfund for Holbæk Amt 65. 41ff.

Riis, P.J. 1993. Ancient Types of Garments. Prolegomena to the Study of Greek and Roman Clothing. Acta Archaeologica 64:2. 149ff.

Rindel, P.O. 1993. Bønder fra stenalder til middelalder ved Nørre Holsted. Nye arkæologiske undersøgelser på den kommende motorvej mellem Vejen og Holsted. Mark og Montre. Årbog for Kunst- og Kulturhistorie. Udgivet af Ribe Amts Museumsråd. 1993. 19ff.

Sandars, N.K. (ed.). 1960. The Epic of Gilgamesh. An English Version with an Introduction. Harmondsworth (Penguin).

van der Sanden, W. 1996. Udødeliggjorte i mosen. Historierne om de nordvesteuropæiske moselig. Amsterdam (Batavian Lion International).

van der Sanden, W.A.B. (ed.). 1990. Mens en moeras. Veenlijken in Nederland van de bronstijd tot en met de Romeinse tijd. Archeologische Monografieën van het Drents Museum 1. Assen (Drents Museum).

Sarauw, T. 2006. Bejsebakken. Late Neolithic Houses and Settlement Structures. Nordiske Fortidsminder. Series C:4. Copenhagen (Det Kongelige Nordiske Oldskriftselskab).

Schauer, P. 1985. Spuren orientalischen und ägäischen Einflusses im bronzezeitlichen Nordischen Kreis. Jahrbuch des Römisch-Germanischen Zentralmuseum 32. 123ff.

Scherping, R. & J.-P. Schmidt. 2007. Seide im Norden – Die Textil-reste am älterbronzezeitlichen Halskragen vom Thürkow, Lkr. Güstrow (Mecklenburg-Vorpommern). Archäologisches Korrespondenzblatt 37:2. 207ff.

Schlabow, K. 1938. Textilreste vom Galgenberg in Itzehoe. Offa 3. 85ff.

————. 1959. Beiträge zur Erforschung der jungsteinzeitlichen und bronzezeitlichen Gewerbetechnik Mitteldeutschlands. Jahresschrift für mitteldeutsche Vorgeschichte 43. 101ff.

———. 1974. Vor- und Frühgeschichtliche Textilfunde aus dem nördlichen Niederlanden. Palaeohistoria. Acta et communicationes instituti bio-archaeologici universitatis Groninganae XVI. 169ff.

———. c1974. Die geborgene Gewerbe aus dem Baumsarg von Harrislee. Manuscript.

Schmidt, J.-P. 2004. Überraschung auf der Erdgastrasse – Bronzezeitliche Gräber in Thürkow. Jöns & Lüth 2004. 126ff.

———. 2007. Die älterbronzezeitlichen Gräber von Thürkow, Lkr. Güstrow. Bodendenkmalpflege in Mecklenburg-Vorpommern 55. 67ff.

Schoeser, M. 2003. World Textiles. A Concise History. London (Thames & Hudson).

Schubart, H. 1972. Die Funde der älteren Bronzezeit in Mecklenburg. Offa-Bücher 26.

Schumacher-Matthäus, G. 1985. Studien zu bronzezeitlichen Schmucktrachten im Karpatenbecken. Ein Beitrag zur Deutung der Hortfunde im Karpatenbecken. Marburger Studien zur Vor- und Frühgeschichte 6. Mainz am Rhein (von Zabern).

Sehested, N.F.B. 1884. Archæologiske Undersøgelser 1878-1881. Kjøbenhavn (Reitzel).

Sherratt, A. 1997. Economy and Society in Prehistoric Europe. Changing Perspectives. Edinburgh (University Press).

Sidrys, R.V. & A. Luchtanas. 1999. Shining Axes, Spiral Pins. Metal Consumption in the East Baltic. Acta Archaeologica 70. 165ff.

Sprockhoff, E. 1939. Ein Frauengrab der älteren Bronzezeit von Lübz. Heimatbund Mecklenburg. Landesverein des Deutschen Heimatbundes 34:2. (Festschrift Robert Beltz.) 101ff.

———. 1954. Nordische Bronzezeit und frühes Griechentum. Jahrbuch des römisch-germanischen Zentralmuseums Mainz 1. 28ff.

Stahlhofen, H. 1978. Eine spätbronzezeitliche Webstuhlgrube in Wallwitz, Kr. Burg. Ausgrabungen und Funde 23. 179ff.

Stieglitz, R.R. 1979. Commodity Prices at Ugarit. Journal of the American Oriental Society 99:1. 15ff.

Stjernquist, B. 1961. Simris II. Bronze Age Problems in the Light of the Simris Excavation. Acta Archaeologica Lundensia Series in 4°:5.

Stöckli, W.E., U. Niffeler & E. Gross-Klee (eds). 1995. Die Schweiz

Bibliography

vom Paläolithikum bis zum frühen Mittelalter. (SPM) II. Basel (Schweizerische Gesellschaft für Ur- und Frühgeschichte).

Strömberg, M. 1973-74. Untersuchungen zur Bronzezeit in Südostschonen. Probleme um die Besiedlung. Meddelanden från Lunds Universitets Historiska Museum. 101ff.

———. 1975. Bronsålder på Österlen. Lund (Kulturnämnden i Ystad).

Thomsen, T. 1929-35. Egekistefundet fra Egtved fra den ældre Bronzealder. Nordiske Fortidsminder II. 165ff. København (Det Kongelige Nordiske Oldskriftselskab/Gyldendal).

Thrane, H. 1962. Hjulgraven fra Storehøj ved Tobøl i Ribe Amt. Kuml 1962. 80ff.

———. 1975a. Europæiske forbindelser. Bidrag til studiet af fremmede forbindelser i Danmarks yngre broncealder (periode IV-V). Nationalmuseets skrifter. Arkæologisk-historisk række XVI. København (Nationalmuseet).

———. 1975b. Fynske broncemennesker fra jernalderen. Fynske Minder 1975. 7ff.

———. 1983. Hoards of the Danish Late Bronze Age (Mont. V). Third Set. Inventaria Archaeologica. Denmark. 9. Set. DK 45. Bonn (Habelt).

———. 1984. Lusehøj ved Voldtofte. En sydvestfynsk storhøj fra yngre bronzealder. Fynske Studier XIII. Odense (Odense Bys Museer).

———. 2004. Fyns Yngre Broncealdergrave 1-2. Fynske Studier 2. Odense (Odense Bys Museer/Syddansk Universitetsforlag).

Tidow, K. 1992. Wollgewebe aus dem bronzezeitlichen Baumsargfund von Harrislee bei Flensburg. Bender Jørgensen & Munksgaard 1992. 31ff.

Toivari-Viitala, J. 2001. Women at Deir el-Medina. A Study of the Status and Roles of the Female Inhabitants in the Workmen's Community during the Ramesside Period. Egyptologische Uitgaven 15. Leiden (Nederlands Instituut voor het Nabije Oosten).

Vargyas, P. 1986. Trade and Prices in Ugarit. Oikumene. Studia ad historiam antiquam classicam et orientalem spectantia 5. 103ff. Budapest (Akadémiai).

Ventris, M.G.F. & J. Chatwick. 1956. Documents in Mycenean Greek. Cambridge (Cambridge University Press).

Vladár, J. 1973. Osteuropäische und mediterrane Einflüsse im Gebiet der Slowakei während der Bronzezeit. Slovenská Archeológia XXI:2. 253ff.

Vogt, E. 1937. Geflechte und Gewebe der Steinzeit. Monographien zur

Bibliography

Ur- und Frühgeschichte der Schweiz I. Basel (Birkhäuser/Schweizerische Gesellschaft für Urgeschichte).

Vons-Comis, S.Y. 1990. De wollen kleding. van der Sanden 1990. 181ff.

Wagner-Hasel, B. 2007. Der Stoff der Macht – Kleidenaufwand, elitärer Konsum und Homerische Königtum. Alram-Stern & Nightingale 2007. 325ff.

Wanzek, B. 1997. Nordica im bronzezeitlichen Südosteuropa. Becker et al. 1997. 527ff.

Wels-Weyrauch, U. 1989. Mittelbronzezeitliche Frauentrachten in Süddeutschland (Beziehungen zur Hagenauer Gruppierung). Dynamique du Bronze moyen en Europe occidentale. Actes du 113e Congrès National des Sociétés Savanters. Strassbourg 1988. Paris (Editions du CTHS). 117ff.

———. 1994. Im Grab erhalten, im Leben getragen – Tracht und Schmuck der Frau. Jochenhövel & Kubach 1994. 59ff.

Willroth, K-H. 1989. Nogle betragtninger over de regionale forhold i Slesvig og Holsten i bronzealderens periode II. Poulsen 1989. 89ff.

Young, G.D. (ed.). 1981. Ugarit in Retrospect. 50 Years of Ugarit and Ugaritic. Proceedings of the Symposium of the same Title held at the University of Wisconsin at Madison, Feb. 26, 1979. Under Auspices of the Middle East Branch of the American Oriental Society and the Mid-West Region of the Society of Biblical literature. Winona Lake (Eisenbrauns).

Glossary

Aegean = Southern Greece. The Aegean Middle and Late Bronze Age sees fine palace centres like Knossos on Crete and Myceanae and Pylos on the Peloponnese, as well as magnificent princely graves and many fine artefacts. Writing is in the Linear B alphabet in the late phase.

Bell-beaker Culture, see **Copper Age**.

blouse, or T-shirt = Female garment of the Bronze Age, rather short and with slightly shortened sleeves, straight neck.

bonnet, or **cap** = female Bronze Age cover for the hair and upper head, with strings.

Bronze Age = archaeological age between the Stone Age and the Iron Age in Old World archaeology. In the Mediterranean the Bronze Age comprises the third and second millennia BC and is divided into Early (third millennium), Middle (around 2000 BC and early second millennium BC), and Late (mid-to late second millennium BC). In Central Europe the Bronze Age starts in the late third millennium BC and ends with the first quarter of the first millennium BC; the Early Bronze Age ends with the first quarter of the second millennium BC; the Middle Bronze Age ends around 1300 BC. The Nordic Bronze Age is divided into two phases (in addition to six main periods), the Early Bronze Age (Periods I-III) starting in the second quarter of the second millennium BC and lasting till *c.* 1100 BC, and Late Bronze Age (Periods IV-VI) lasting till 500 BC. The full Nordic Bronze Age dresses are of the fourteenth to thirteenth centuries BC, Periods II-III of the Early Bronze Age.

cloak = large male Bronze Age garment worn over the one or both shoulders, either oval and smaller, or kidney-shaped and larger.

coat = male Bronze Age garment covering abdomen (to about the knees), breast and back, with one point over the shoulder.

Copper Age = archaeological period in the fifth millennium BC in the Balkans which saw attempts to raise the cultural level in areas such as pottery technology, metallurgy and even symbolic communication (non-administrative writing). The term is also used for culture groups with metallurgy dating to just before the Bronze Age, for instance the Bell-beaker Culture (Western and Central Europe).

foot wrap = piece of cloth serving as a sock in leather shoes.

ground loom = simple horizontal loom using sticks stuck into the ground to hold horizontal sticks and the warp threads. Cf. warp-weighted loom and tubular loom for heddle and shed rods, etc.

hair net = Bronze Age female garment either with long thick strings for fastening it on the head in frontlet fashion (including a string under the chin), or in the form of a very light bonnet (q.v.).

Hittites = Nation dominating (eastern) Anatolia (in Turkey) in the Late Bronze Age.

Iron Age (see also **Bronze Age**) = the archaeological age after the Bronze Age. In the North, the Iron Age is divided into a so-called Pre-Roman (or Celtic) phase, 500-0 BC, following the European development. An (Imperial) Roman Iron Age is dated to 0-400 AD. This is followed by the Migration or Germanic period, and the Viking Age, till around 1000 AD.

loincloth = male Bronze Age garment covering the abdomen only (reaches to about the knees).

large skirt = archaic term for a wrap (q.v.). Since the lower body of some women were covered by this garment in the grave, and even belted, it has been mistaken for a skirt, but is too large for such a use.

loom = instrument for joining warp (q.v.) thread with weft (q.v.) ones; primitive looms come in several main types (q.v.): ground loom, warp-weighted loom, tubular loom, etc. Tablet weave (q.v.) is made on a loom only made up of tablets.

loom-weight = weight to stretch the warp threads on a warp-weighed loom (see this).

napkin = piece of cloth; by women used belted during menstruation, or for other purposes.

Neolithic = Stone Age, usually with little evidence of metal.

net bag or **'shopping bag'** = female piece of textile identified by the present author, previously taken to be a truly transparent string skirt.

pixie-cap = male Bronze Age cap of normal thickness.

plain skirt = female garment covering the abdomen, reaching to between below the knees to the ankles.

plain weave, see **tabby**.

ritual 'T-shirt' = male bronze Age garment hanging from the shoulders in two V-shaped tongues covering the crotch and buttocks like a breechcloth, but open to the sides.

rock-carving = Bronze Age images carved on natural rock or on large stones.

skirt = garment covering the lower part of the body, which in the Bronze Age comes in two varieties: string skirt (q.v.) or plain skirt (q.v.).

spindle = instrument for producing threads (of wool).

spindle-whorl = whorl at the lower end of a spindle to give it momentum.

spinning = drawing out of cleaned, that is carded, wool for making a thread by turning a spindle, includes twisting the thread either to the right, producing a so-called Z-thread, or to the left, producing a so-called S-thread.

Stone Age, see **Neolithic** and **Bronze Age**.

string skirt = female skirt made of strings and in the Bronze Age wound twice around the body. The strings are fastened both at the top (waist) and at the bottom, making the skirt much less transparent than often believed; it reaches to just above the knees. According to figurines displaying cultic dance some string-skirts were very short indeed, covering only the top of the thighs.

tabby, or **plain weave** = simplest weave, consisting of alternating over and under passes of the weft; the warp and the weft threads are usually of nearly the same diameter.

tablet weave = simple weaving technique using small tablets with holes as a loom to produce long strips of cloth (which may be joined to make for larger garments).

T-shirt, see **blouse**.

tubular loom = loom usually with uprights and two horizontal beams. Cf. **ground loom** and **warp-weighted loom** for heddle and shed rods, etc.

twill = complex weave that aims at producing diagonal lines, thus patterns in the fabric.

war cap = Bronze Age thick, well-made male skull cap, or helmet.

warp = tensioned threads, in warp-weighted looms fastened to the upper horizontal beam.

warp-weighted loom = upright loom essentially consisting of a frame of two uprights and an upper beam, plus a heddle rod secured by loops to lift every second warp thread, for instance, thus overruling the action of the shed rod. The upper beam may be rolled as the work goes along, thus accommodating longer pieces of cloth. Cf. **ground loom** and **tubular loom**.

weft = non-tensioned threads in loom weaving.

wrap = vary large rectangular piece of cloth used by females as an outer garment and for other purposes (traditionally often termed a 'blanket', even a 'large skirt').

Tables

Table 1. Dendro-dated oak-coffin graves from the Early Bronze Age with well preserved garments. M = Male; F = Female. Based on Randsborg & Christensen 2006.

A male grave of Initial Period II from Sønder Ønlev (AK VI3028) is dendro-dated to 'some time' after c. 1468 BC. Borum Eshøj grave B is the latest dendro-dated grave from Period II. The earliest dendro-dated Period III grave is from c. 1319 BC. The transition between Period II and Period III is thus dendro-dated to around 1330 BC. Unfortunately, the famous female Skrydstrup Grave is merely C-14 dated (and likely of Period III).

	Reference	Archaeological period	Dendro-date (BC)
Guldhøj:A M	AK VIII3820	Early Period II	c. 1377/likely 1389
Store Kongshøj:A M	AK VIII3832A	Early Period II	c. 1385
Lille Dragshøj M	AK VI2878	Period II	c. 1375-70
Egtved F	AK IX4357	Early (?) Period II	1370
Muldbjerg M	AK X4740	Early/Late Period II*	1365
Trindhøj:A M	AK VII3817	Late Period II*	after c. 1355
Arildshøj M	AKIV2243	(Late) Period II	shortly after c. 1349
Borum Eshøj:A M – the old man	Boye 1896, 49f.	Period II	c. 1348
Jels M	AK VII3443	Late (?) Period II	likely 1348
Borum Eshøj:B M – the young man	Boye 1896, 49f.	Late Period II*	c. 1344
Nybøl M	AK VI3022	Period III	c. 1266

*Grave holds Central European imports of Middle Bronze Age Period Reinecke C2

Table 2. Quality of Early Bronze Age cloth: average number of threads (warp/weft) per centimetre of various Early Bronze Age garments (Broholm & Hald 1929-35, 330; Broholm 1939, 49f. (M. Hald); Bender Jørgensen, Munksgaard & Stærmose Nielsen 1982; Tidow 1992 cf. Schlabow c. 1974); recalculated and simplified.

Males are listed at the top, females below; the present terminology for dress items applies. P = pixie cap. Melhøj is of Period III, Skrydstrup likely the same; the rest are of Period II. For particular references, see Tables 5 & 7. For comparison, the female Borremose garment in twill (ninth century, or mid-Late Bronze Age) is listed below the female group (cf. Hald 1980, 20f.). There are no differences in terms of quality of cloth between genders. Dress items worn close to the body may be of finer cloth than other garments.

	Cloak	Coat	Sheet/blanket	Foot-wrappings	Other
Arildshøj	–	? (4/4)	4/4	–	–
Lille	(present)	–	5/4	5/4 & 4/4	4/3 (P)
Dragshøj	(present)	–	(sheet/blanket?)	(foot-wrappings?)	–
Toppehøj	–	–	–	–	4/3 & 4/4
Jels	–	–	–	–	4/3 (P)
Trindhøj	4/3	4/3	5/4	6/4	4/3 (P)
Guldhøj	4/3	4/3	4/3	5/5	4/3 (P)
Muldbjerg	4/3	4/3	4/3	4/3	–
Borum Eshøj					
– old man	4/3	4/4	–	4/3	–
– young man	4/3	4/4	–	–	–

Table 2 (continued)

	T-shirt	Skirt (string)	Wrap	Foot-wrappings	Other
Egtved	4/3		4/3	4/3	4/3 (cremation cloth) ?
Borum Eshøj – old woman	4/3	5/3 & 4/3 (2 skirts?)	4/3	–	
Skrydstrup	4/4 (5/3 = piecing)	5/3 & 4/4 (2 skirts)	5/4	4/3 (& 4/3?)	(present)
Melhøj	8/5	5/3	(present)	–	–
Borremose	-	6/5	–	–	–

Table 3. Distribution of warp-threads per centimetre in fragments of Bronze Age textiles that have survived in graves as a result of the presence of metal-oxides. (Calculated Late Bronze Age percentages are quite small.) After Randsborg & Christensen 2006; data Bender Jørgensen 1986.

Threads/cm:	1-5	6-10	>10	Σ
Early Bronze Age Period II	74 (64%)	32 (28%)	9 (8%)	115
Early Bronze Age Period III	32 (46%)	32 (46%)	6 (9%)	70
Late Bronze Age	11 (46%)	3 (13%)	10 (42%)	24
Σ	117	67	25	209

Table 4. Spinning directions of Early Bronze Age cloth: warp/weft – left (S)/right (Z), or other combinations (Broholm & Hald 1929-35, 330; Tidow 1992, cf. Schlabow c. 1974); recalculated and simplified. Nos of measurements indicated.

Males are listed at the top, females below; the new terminology for dress items used in this book applies. P = pixie cap. Melhøj is of Period III, Skrydstrup likely the same; the rest are of Period II. For particular references, see Tables 5 & 7. For comparison, the female Borremose garment in twill (ninth century, or Late Bronze Age) is listed below the female group (cf. Hald 1980, 20f.).

As expected, there is no difference in terms of spinning directions between male and female garments.

	Cloak	Coat	Sheet/blanket	Foot-wrappings	Other
Arildshøj	–	? (S/Z)	c. 3 S/Z	1 S/S & 1 S/S (foot-wrappings?)	1 S/Z (P)
Lille Dragshøj	(present)	–	2 S/Z (sheet/blanket?)		
Toppehøj	(present)	–	–	–	1 S/Z & 1 S/Z
Jels	–	–	–	–	6 ?/? (P)
Trindhøj	2 S/Z	4 S/Z	6 S/Z	2 S/Z	1 S/Z (P)
Guldhøj	3 S/S	2 S/Z	1 S/S	2 S/S	2 S/Z (P)
Muldbjerg	2 S/Z	6 S/Z / 1 S/S	1 S/Z	1 S/Z	–
Borum Eshøj					
– old man	8 S/S	6 S/Z	–	2 S/?	–
– young man	6 S/Z	5 S/Z	–	–	–

Table 4 (continued)

	T-shirt	Skirt	Wrap	Foot-wrappings	Other
Egtved	4 S/Z 1 S/S	(string)	9 S/Z	4 S/S	1 S/Z (cremation cloth)
Borum Eshøj – old woman	3 S/Z	1 S/Z & 1 S/Z (2 skirts?)	1 S/Z	–	?
Skrydstrup	3 S/Z (1 S/Z = piecing)	2 S/S & 2 S/Z (2 skirts)	4 S/Z	1 Z/S (?) (1 Z/S (?))	(present)
Melhøj	7 S/S	40 S/S&Z	(present)	–	–
Borremose	–	? S/S	–	–	–

143

Table 5. Women of the Early Bronze Age: dress items quoted in new terminology, with accessories. All measurements are in cm (Boye 1896; Thomsen 1929-35; Broholm & Hald 1929-35; 1939; cf. Amer & Kersten 1973ff.; Hvass 1981; Randsborg & Christensen 2006). The Late Bronze Age (likely Period V) Borremose bog body is added (van der Sanden 1996, 195 no. 115 (with further references); Jensen 2002, 389f.; Hald 1980). S = shoes (remains); F = foot-wrappings (cf. Hald 1972, 11ff.). Several graves, most without remnants of preserved textiles but with bronze sheet metal tubes indicating the presence of a string skirt, are added below; more might have been added (cf. Randsborg & Nybo 1984, 175; Strömberg 1973-74; Oldeberg 1974). String skirts with bronze tubes are seemingly unknown towards the southwest of the overall region, with its rather more modest investment in bronzes in female graves.

Grave	Age	Height	Blouse	Skirt; Shoes; Foot-wrappings; Headgear	Wrap	Accessories
Egtved (AK 4357)	c. 17	160	T	string F	258x 192*	ear-ring, belt-plate, 2 bracelets, comb [cremated bones of a child, c. 5 years]
Borum Eshøj – old woman (DBI, 791)	50-60	156	T	likely present bonnet	330x 122**	necklace, fibula, belt-plate, dagger, 2 bracelets, 2 tutuli, 2 finger spirals, comb
Skrydstrup • (AK 3527;A)	c. 17	171	T	161x125* & 193x106* S F hairnet bonnet	390x 116**	2 gold ear-spirals, comb

Table 5 (continued)

Melhøj● (DBI, 1862)	?	□150	?	present (not string)	present	2 gold ear-spirals, necklace, 2 fibulae, dagger, ferrule, 2 bracelets, belt-plate, tutulus, ankle ring
Hvilshøj†● (AK 5340)	?	?	?	hairnet	present***	necklace, comb
Ginderup● (AK 5451;A)	?	?	?	string	likely	necklace, fibula, fingering, 2 bracelets, double-button
Borremose (9th century BC)	20-35	>143	None	183x 121	none	none
Sonnerup (AK 228)	?	?	?	string	?	belt-plate, tutulus, many tubes (for string skirt)
Melby (AK 243I)	?	?	?	string	?	neck collar, dagger, 3 tutuli, glass bead, 2 amber beads, tubes (for string skirt)
Veksø (AK284;B)	30-40	?	?	string	?	fibula, amber bead, tubes (for string skirt)
Ølby (AK 299)	30-40	180	?	string	?	neck collar, belt-plate, dagger (ex-sword blade), 4 tutuli (3 bossed), glass bead, 2 amber beads, spirals, many tubes (for string skirt)

145

Table 5 (continued)

Grave	Age	Height	Blouse	Skirt; Shoes; Foot-wrappings; Headgear	Wrap	Accessories
Vester Såby (AK 578;A)	?	?	?	string	?	gold ear-rings, knife, many tubes (for string skirt)[+]
Svallerup[++] (AK 626;D)	?	?	?	string	?	neck-collar, fibula, 4 tutuli. 2 bracelets, 5 tubes and spiral tubes (for string skirt), [bracelet, spiral ring]
Hagendrup (AK 976)	?	?	?	string	?	neck-collar, belt-plate, several tubes (for string skirt), [etc.]
Tårnholm (AK 1163;A)	?	?	?	string	?	neck collar, tutulus, belt-plate, dagger, 2 bracelets, finger spirals, tubes (for string skirt), [tutulus]
Olsker (AK 1454;B)	?	?	?	string	?	Bornholm fibula, many tubes (for string skirt), 2 bracelets, 2 double-buttons, knife

Table 5 (continued)

Loftsgård+ (AK 1477;IVA)	?	?	string?	?	Bornholm fibula, tube (for string skirt?), spiral tubes, finger-ring, several small hooks (for garment or bag?), many glass beads, beads of bronze and amber, tutulus, double-button, vessel
Gyldensgård (AK 1550)	?	?	string	?	numerous tubes (for string skirt)
Ravnsby (AK 1655;A)	?	?	string	?	belt plate, dagger, awl, several tubes (for string skirt)
Hverrehus (DBI, 728)	c. 20	?	string	?	neck collar, belt-plate, 14 tutuli, dagger, comb of bronze, 4 bracelets, many tubes (for string skirt)
Bustrup (DBI, 741)	20-25	?	string	?	necklace, animal tooth beads (1 pig, 3 dog), belt-plate, dagger (scabbard with ferrule), tubes (for string skirt), clay pot, clay cup, [various textiles]

Table 5 (continued)

Grave	Age	Height	Blouse	Skirt; Shoes; Foot-wrappings; Headgear	Wrap	Accessories
Nimtofte (DBI, 773)	?	?	?	string	?	neck-collar (?), arm rings, finger-rings, several bronze tubes (for string skirt), cup
Store Købinge● (Oldeberg 1974, No. 753)	?	?	?	string	?	gold spiral ring, knife, spiral bracelets, many tubes (for string skirt), double-button, etc.
Vallebjerg (Strömberg 1973-74, 110f.)	?	?	?	string	?	belt-plate, spiral bracelets, many tubes (for string skirt)

* Over the dressed body as a blanket.
** Wrapped around the dressed body like a sheet and blanket; short ends coarsely joined by tacking.
*** On top of the cremated bones.
+ Cremation.
++ Cremation, one of the very rare ones of this period.
● Period III (the unmarked graves are Period II)

148

Table 6. Women of the Early Bronze Age: Summary and interpretations of Table 5.
Several graves without textiles but with bronze tubes indicating the presence of a string skirt are added below; several more might have been listed (cf. Randsborg & Nybo 1984, 175). The blouses are of a little less than 0.75 m² cloth each. The Late Bronze Age (likely Period V) Borremose bog body is added (van der Sanden 1996, 195 no. 115 (with further references); Jensen 2002, 389f.; Hald 1980).

Grave	Age	Blouse	Skirt m²	Wrap m²	Accessories (selection)	Suggested status	Period of burial
Egtved	c. 17	T	string (0.6)	5.0	belt-plate (plain)	junior cult member, unmarried,	early Sept
Borum Eshøj	50-60	T	(likely)	4.0	necklace, fibula, belt-plate (plain), dagger	senior cult member, married, high rank	mid March, or end Sept
Skrydstrup	c. 17	T	2.0 & 2.0/1.9	4.5	2 gold ear-spirals	unmarried, high rank	end Sept
Melhøj* or	?	T	not	(large)	2 gold ear-	senior cult	early May,
			string		spirals, belt-plate, dagger, 2 fibulae	member, married, high rank	early Aug
Hvilshøj*	?	?	present	?	necklace	married, rank?	late April, or mid Aug?
Ginderup*	?	?	string	likely	necklace, fibula, bracelets	married, rank?	?

149

Table 6 (continued)

Grave	Age	Blouse	Skirt m²	Wrap m²	Accessories (selection)	Suggested status	Period of burial
Borremose 9th century BC	20-35	–	2.2	–	–	high?	winter
Sønnerup	?	?	string	?	belt-plate	cult member	?
Melby	?	?	string	?	neck collar, dagger, glass bead	married, high rank	early April, or early Sept
Veksø	30-40	?	string	?	fibula	cult member, low rank	mid April, or late August
Ølby	30-40	?	string	?	neck collar, belt-plate (likely plain), dagger, bossed tutuli, glass bead	senior cult member, married, high rank	(early May, or early August?)
Vester Såby	?	?	string	?	gold ear-rings[+]	junior cult member, high rank	?
Svallerup**	?	?	string	?	neck-collar, fibula, tutuli, bracelets	married	?

150

Table 6 (continued)

Hagendrup	?	?	string	?	neck collar, belt-plate	senior cult member, married	?
Tårnholm	?	?	string	?	neck collar, belt-plate (plain), dagger	senior cult member, married	late March, or late Sept
Olsker	?	?	string	?	Bornholm fibula, knife bracelets	senior cult member, married, high rank	?
Loftsgård*	?	?	string	?	Bornholm fibula, many glass beads	senior cult member high rank	?
Gyldensgård	?	?	string	?	many tubes	unmarried? high rank?	?
Ravnsby	?	?	string	?	belt-plate, dagger	senior cult member, married, low rank	mid March, or end Sept

Table 6 (continued)

Grave	Age	Blouse	Skirt m²	Wrap m²	Accessories (selection)	Suggested status	Period of burial
Hverrehus	c. 20+	?	string	?	neck collar, belt-plate (calendar), many tutuli, dagger, bronze comb, 4 bracelets	senior cult member, married, high rank	?
Bustrup	20-25	?	string	?	necklace, dagger	married	early March, or mid Oct
Nimtofte	?	?	string	?	neck collar? arm rings	married?	?
Store Købinge*	?	?	string	?	gold spiral ring, bracelets, many tubes	unmarried, high rank	(spring/ autumn)
Vallebjerg	?	?	string	?	belt-plate, bracelets, many tubes	cult member, low rank	late March, or late Sept

* Period III
** Cremation (one of the very rare ones of this period)

152

Table 7. Men of the Early Bronze Age: preserved dress items, etc. The measures of the cloaks are maximum sizes, before rounding the edges by cutting away cloth; all measurements are in cm (Boye 1896; Broholm & Hald 1929-35; cf. Aner & Kersten 1973ff; Randsborg & Christensen 2006; etc.). The caps are listed as WC = war cap (heavy, thick 'helmet') and P = pixie cap (thin, ordinary). S = shoes (remains); F = foot-wrappings (cf. Hald 1972, 11ff). Nybøl (AK 3022) is Period III, all other graves are Period II. Addition (below): Bredhøj which is probably male (AK4815A).

Grave	Cap; Shoes; Foot-wrappings	Cloak	m^2	Coat/loincloth	m^2	Sheet/blanket	m^2	Period of burial
Arildshøj (AK 2243)	WC	–	–	?		142+x43+	>0.6	end April, or mid-August
Lille Dragshøj (AK 2878)	WC	cloak		?		–		mid-March, or late Sept/early Oct
Toppehøj (AK 3006)	WC	cloak (?)		?		–		mid-Jan, or early Dec
Nybøl (AK 3022)	? *(1)*	?		?		+	?	? (NNW-SSE)
Jels (AK 3443)	P S	?		?		–		mid-March, or early Oct

Table 7 (continued)

Grave	Cap; Shoes; Foot-wrappings	Cloak	m²	Coat/loincloth	m²	Sheet/blanket	m²	Period of burial
Trindhøj (AK 3817)	WC P S F	243x126	<3.1	134x107	1.4	184x133**	2.4	mid-Feb, or late Oct
Guldhøj (AK 3820)	WC P (cut) S F F	c. 205x125	<c. 2.6	(present)	?	–		mid-April, or late August
Store Konigshøj (AK 3832A)	WC	likely		?		–		late Feb, or late Oct
Muldbjerg (AK 4740)	WC F	231x118	<2.7	135x94	1.3	131x211*	2.8	mid-Jan, or late Nov

154

Table 7 (continued)

Borum Eshøj							
– old man (Boye 49f.; DB I, 789)	WC	195x104	<2.0	123x78	1.0	–	early March, or early Oct
– young man+ (Boye 49f.; DB I, 790)	F *no cap* S?	191x108	<2.1	115+x75	0.9	–	? (N-S; head in south; burial mid-winter?)
Bredhøj (AK 4815A)	? (2)	?		?		?	mid-March, or early Oct

* Under the dressed body, as a sheet
** White, fringed; cut in two pieces: under the head and around the feet
+ Significantly, no war cap
(1) Breechcloth (?)
(2) Broad belt (?) in open-work

155

Table 8. Women of the Early and Late Bronze Age: dress items quoted in the new terminology (cf. Tables 4f.). At the foot of the table the following are given: size of present-day cotton cloth used for dresses and baby-carriers in West Africa (Bénin) (cf. Fig. 19), as well as of a traditional burial cloth (example); an example of the prestigious Kente cloth from Ghana); a traditional Scottish plaid. All cloth measurements are in cm.

Grave	Wrap	m²	Skirt	m²
Egtved	258x192 *wrap worn as a double skirt**	5.0	string c. 154x38 *192x129*	0.6 *2.5*
Borum Eshøj – old woman	330x122 *wrap worn as a double skirt***	4.0	(likely present) *165x122*	? *2.0*
Skrydstrup	390x116 *wrap worn as a double skirt***	4.5	161x125 & 193/179x106 *195x116*	2.0 & 2.0/1.9*** *2.3*
Melhøj+	present	–	present	–
Hvilshøj+●	?	–	present	–
Borremose (9th century BC)	–		183x121	2.2

Table 8 (continued)

Bénin
– woman's skirt   170x115   2.0
– burial wrap****   457x c. 95?   c. 4.3

Ghana
– Kente cloth*****   180x179   3.2

Scotland: Islay
– traditional plaid   170x150   2.6
  (same size as cloak)

+ Period III
• Cremation
* Just possible to wear as skirt
** Not possible to wear as skirt, opens at the waist
*** Sum 4.0/3.9
**** 'Five yards', Kingdom of Dahomey (Herskovits 1938/I, 371)
***** Male ceremonial garment (Blier 1998, 150)

Table 9. *Top of table*: Women of the Early Bronze Age: belts, strings, and 'towels' (lengths in cm); likely sanitary belts and napkins or towels. Cf. Table 4. *Centre (Nybøl)*: possibly male breechcloth (Period III). *Foot of table*: sanitary napkins from ancient recent times (for Ancient Egypt: Toivari-Viitala 2001; McDowell 2002). Italics = width and length as worn.

Grave	Belt/(string) (length in cm)	Napkin	m^2
Egtved	c. 175 (tassels)+	27x97/20x110*	0.26/0.22
	245 (string)	9x97/7x110	0.09/0.08
		– folded 3x width	
		9x49/7x55	0.04/0.04
		– folded 3x width	
		& 1x length	
Borum Eshøj – old woman	246 (tassels)	27x48 (thick)	0.13
	204 (no tassels)	9x48	0.04
		– folded 3x width	
Skrydstrup	215 (no tassels)	31x39	0.12
		10x39	0.04
		– folded 3x width	
Nybøl (AK 3022)		9½x97+++	0.09

Table 10. Consumption of textiles, main garments: selected female and male graves (cf. Tables 5-7, etc.). Caps, bonnets, belts, etc. are merely listed, not included in the calculations. WC = war cap, P = pixie cap. B = belt (S = string). F = foot-wrappings. Leather items (belts, shoes) are not listed.

Female

Grave	Head-dress; Belt; Foot-wrappings	m²	Blouse m²	Skirt m²	Wrap m²	Other m²	Σm² (approx)
Egtved	B F*	0.2	0.7	string 0.6	5.0	napkin 0.2	6.7
Borum Eshøj – old woman	bonnet /hairnet 2B	0.1	0.7	likely** [>>0.2]	4.0	napkin 0.1 net bag	>5.1***
Skrydstrup	bonnet & hairnet B F	0.2 0.1	0.7	2.0 & 2.0/1.9	4.5	napkin 0.1	9.6

Table 10 (continued)

Male Grave	Head-dress; Belt; Foot-wrappings	m²	Cloak m²	Coat m²/loincloth	Sheet m²/blanket	Other m²	Σm² (approx)
Trindhøj	WC P BF	0.1	<3.1	1.4	2.4	–	7.0
Guldhøj	WC P (cut) F	?	<2.6	?	–	–	>>2.6$^+$
Muldbjerg	WC F	0.2	<2.7	1.3	2.8	–	7.0
Borum Eshøj – old man	WC S F	0.1	<2.0	1.0	–	–	3.1
– young man	[No cap, no F]		<2.1	0.9	–	–	3.0

* 4 specimens (triangular), including one or two pieces seemingly left over from making a male oval cloak (cf. Eskildsen & Lomborg 1977); remains of cloth were also found at the knees (Alexandersen et al. 1981, 35f. Fig. 8)
** 2 skirts?   *** c. 7.0 m² with one long skirt, c. 9.0 m² with two long skirts
$^+$ At least c. 4.0 m² with a coat (coat or loincloth obligatory). c. 6.5 m² with a sheet/blanket too

Table 11. Dress items & accessories, and emphasised body parts and movements. Cf. Table 12.
Top: naked female bronze figurines (no tenons).
Centre: Male and female bronze figurines from larger composite representations (tenons on feet), plus heads of figures, for instance on knives.
Foot: human beings depicted on bronzes, in particular razors (cf. Kaul 1998).

	Male dress	Male body	Female dress	Female body
Head			earring	
Neck			necklace(s)	
Arms				
Torso				breasts (small)
Abdomen			belt (etc.)	vagina
Legs				
Feet				
Movement				standing
Head	pointed hat, horned helmet, mask		earring	hairdo, incl. pony tail eyes
Neck			necklace(s)	
Arms	cult axe		bracelet	
Body	V-shirt		T-shirt, fibula	breasts (small)

	Male dress	Male body	Female dress	Female body
Abdomen	loincloth, belt		string & long skirts, belt	
Legs				shin
Feet			shoes	
Movement		standing, seated/dancing		standing, seated/dancing, acrobatics

	Male dress	Male body	Female dress	Female body
Head	rays (sun deity?), horns			pony tail
Neck				
Arms	cult axe, paddle			
Torso				
Abdomen				
Legs		shin		shin
Feet				
Movement		dancing, paddling		standing

162

Table 12. Dress items and accessories, and emphasised body parts and movements: male and female human beings on rock-carvings. Cf. Table 11. Crew strokes on ships are not discussed. The images on rock-carvings are mainly from the provinces of Bohuslän and Østfold, present-day Swedish-Norwegian borderlands on the Kattegat (Cattegat Sea) (cf. Coles 2005).

	Male dress	Male body	Female dress	Female body
Head	pointed hat, horned helmet, bird mask		pony tail	
Neck				
Arms	lur, cult axe, sword, spear, bow, branch, 'wings', sling?		large hands	
Body	cloak, shield/ wheel-cross		body wrap	
Abdomen		phallos		vagina (cup-mark)
Legs		shin		shin
Feet				
Movement		procession (also on board ships, seated/dancing), coitus with woman/animal, handling weapons, fighting & hunting, carrying (model ship or sun image), chariot driving, riding (fighting), acrobat riding, pole jumping, sailing (paddling)		procession, acrobatics

163

Table 13. Seasonally determined burials of man and woman (cf. Tables 6-7). The higher number of women is due to the ease of identifying metal-decorated string skirts, a garment evidently mainly worn in the summer (all are from the period early March to mid-October). The number of string-skirt burials is given in italics below. Men wear heavy war caps (and pixie caps); cloaks (likely all); and loin-cloths (likely all); blankets also occur.

Note that two seasonal values pertain to each horizontal reading. In just a few cases the time of burial is unequivocal, such as for the women of Egtved and Skrydstrup: both September, respectively early and late.

	October-March	April-September	Σ
Men	8*	2	10
Women	3	9	12
Σ	11	11	22
String-skirt	*2½*	*5½*	*8*

*Possibly even 9, if the young man at Borum Eshøj is a winter burial (DB I, 790). ¹Half burials result from uncertainty concerning the season.

Table 14. Suggested archaeological criteria for the evaluation of the status of women (cf. Table 5-6; Randsborg & Christensen 2006). Lack of criteria does not imply lack of particular status. Wealth is a partly independent factor.

senior (married) member of cult group (healers),	neck collar, belt-plate, tutuli, belt-box (Period III, for many amulets), vessel for drink
junior (unmarried) member of cult group	(small) belt-plate and/or tutuli, bracelets, vessel for drink
married status	necklace/neck collar, dagger, 'male' bossed tutuli
unmarried status	bracelets and minor rings (only); sanitary napkin
high rank	elaborate coiffure; gold; many (fine) bronzes, dagger, fibula; glass beads
lower rank	no gold; no exotica; a few bronzes
identified specialists*	weaver; potter; healer; member of cult group; etc.

* weaver and potter merely inferred

165

Table 15. Suggested archaeological criteria for the evaluation of the status of men (cf. Table 7; Randsborg & Christensen 2006). Lack of criteria does not imply lack of particular status. Wealth is a partly independent factor.

royal/commanding rank	war cap; folding chair, chariot stick; fine drinking vessels in metal and wood (studded); gold; heavy weapons/many bronzes, bossed tutuli, fibula, exotica
high member of cult group	special T-shirt; gold-foil sun disc or ceremonial urn (Skallerup model wagon*) at burial, many amulets
high rank	war cap; gold; weapons/bronzes, fibula, exotica
high rank, junior	no war cap; dagger
lower rank	no gold; poor weapons (if any)/few bronzes
identified specialists	commander/charioteer/ship's captain; warrior; bronze and gold craftsman; surgeon; healer; member of cult group; etc.

* AK 1269, Period III

Table 16. *Above:* Catalogue of woollen textile fragments from graves of the Middle Bronze Age (= Nordic Period II) in the Schwarza area, Südthüringen (South Thuringia), Germany. The graves are nearly all female. Fulling is common. The average number of threads per cm is given; as noted, warp/weft spinning directions are almost all S/S (Feustel 1958/K. Schlabow; cf. Farke 1993). The average quality of the cloth preserved, in particular of the light, open 'veil' cloth, a unique product, is clearly higher than in the North (cf. Table 2). This might indicate that the Nordic textiles are local and saw few imports.

Centre: Earlier Bronze Age textiles from Unterteutschenthal, Saxony (Schlabow 1959: seemingly, the first of the fragments has weft threads of flax).

Below: Large textile fragments from Emmer-Erfscheienveen, northeasternmost Netherlands (Vons-Comis 1990); two Period II textile fragments from a grave at Bonstorf, Lower Saxony (Laux 1981-83, 67; Bender Jørgensen 1992, 224); textiles from Period III graves in Mecklenburg (Just 1964: slightly deviating information; Schubart 1972, 94 Grab A1; Bender Jørgensen 1992, 225): Mecklenburg is attached to the Nordic Bronze Age Culture.

Ordinary cloth	Open or 'veil' cloth
6/6 (S/S)	12/6 (Z/Z & S/S)
6/6 (S/S)	7/6 (Z/Z & S/S)
8/8 (S/S)	10/6 (S/S)
7/7 (S/S)	5/5 (S/S)
6/6 (S/S)	
6/7 (S/S)	
4½/4½ (S/S)	
8/6 (S/S)	
10/8 (S/S) *	
Average quality = 7/7	*Average quality = 9/6*

Table 16 (continued)

9/5 (flax) (S/S) – Unterteutschenthal, Saxony
10/5 (S/S) – Unterteutschenthal, Saxony

Average quality = 10/5

Emmer-Erfscheienveen (S/S), northeastern Netherlands

Average quality = 5[4-6]/4

6/6 (Z/S) – Bonsdorf, Lower Saxony
8/6 (Z/S) – Bonsdorf, Lower Saxony

Average quality = 7/6

5/5 (Z/S) – Blengow, Mecklenburg
4/5 (Z/S) – Friedrichsruhe, Mecklenburg
7/7 (Z/S) – Friedrichsruhe, Mecklenburg
6/4 (S/Z?) – Friedrichsruhe, Mecklenburg

Average quality = 6/5

c. 40/8 (Z/Z) – Friedrichsruhe, Mecklenburg (likely a belt)

* The only male interment of the Schwarza group, and the finest one as to the quality of cloth

168

Table 17. *Above:* Middle Bronze Age woollen textiles (largely contemporary with Period II in the North) from the saltworks at Hallstatt in the Austrian Alps (Grömer 2007, Figs 76 & 72). Distribution of number of threads per cm is given.
Below: Types of warp/weft spinning directions and their combinations.

No. of threads per cm	1-5	6-10	11-15	>15	Σ
No. of specimens	26	18	3	2	49 (plus two in linen)

Spinning combinations	S/S	S/Z, Z/S?	Z/Z	S/Z	Z/S	S,Z/S	□
No. of specimens	13	19	11	2	4	2	51
Twills of these	–	*1*	*2*	–	–	–	*3*

169

Table 18. Prices in the Hittite Kingdom (Hoffner 1997). At Ebla, Syria in the late third millennium, 1 x gold = 7-8 x silver = 56-80 x tin (Burney 2004, 229).

1 cheese = 0.5 silver shekel
1 bottle of lard/butter/honey = 1 silver shekel
150 litres wheat = 1 silver shekel
200 litres barley = 0.5 silver shekel
50 litres barley = 0.125 silver shekel
1 ox (meat) = 0.5 silver shekel

Utensils and weapons
1 copper box of 1.5 minas (705g) = 12.5 silver shekels
1 bronze axe of 2 minas (940g) = 0.33 silver shekel
1 copper axe of 1 mina (470g) = 0.125 silver shekel

Garments and grooming
1 (fine) sheet = 15 silver shekels
1 (fine) garment = 3-4-10-12 silver shekels
1 blue wool garment = 20 silver shekels
1 large bolt of linen = 5 silver shekels
1 fine shirt = 3 silver shekels
1 breech-cloth = 5 silver shekels
1 gown = 6 silver shekels
1 thin tunic = 3 silver shekels
1 sheepskin with fleece = 1 silver shekel
1 hide of ox = 1-4 silver shekels

Animals
1 sheep = 1 silver shekel
1 full grown cow = 7 silver shekels
1 plough ox = 12 silver shekels
1 bull = 10 silver shekels
1 draft horse = 20 silver shekels
1 mule = 1 pound silver = 40 silver shekels
1 horse = 14 silver shekel

Slaves and other
Killing of merchant in foreign land = fine of 100 silver minas

Metals (approximate values)
1 Hittite shekel = 11.75g
1 Hittite mina ('pound') = 470g.
4 minas copper = 160 shekel copper (1880 g) = 1 silver shekel (in value)
1 x gold = 7-9 x silver (= 1120-1440 x copper)

Table 19. Prices in New Kingdom Egypt (Janssen 1975).

Foods
   1 sack of wheat (*c.* 58 kg) = 1-2 copper deben
   1 sack of barley = 2 copper deben
   1 loaf of bread = 0.1 copper deben
   50 fish = 2 copper deben
   1 thigh of a cow = *c.* 30 copper deben
   1 litre of beer = ½ copper deben

Utensils and weapons
   1 bronze jar = 1⅔ silver kit = 18 copper deben
   1 bronze cup = 5 copper deben
   1 leather bucket = 3 copper deben
   1 basket = 4 copper deben
   1 big spear = 2 copper deben
   1 normal spear = 1½ copper deben

Garments and grooming
   1 linen sheet = 3⅓ silver kit = 33 copper deben
   10 shirts of fine linen = 4 silver kit
   1 shirt = 2½-5 copper deben
   1 smooth garment (various types) = 10-30 copper deben
   1 pair of sandals = 2 copper deben
   1 razor = 1-2 copper deben
   1 mirror = 6 copper deben
   1 glass bead necklace = 5 copper deben

Furniture and funerals
   1 bed = 12-20 copper deben
   1 chair (etc.) = 13-20 copper deben
   1 table = 15 copper deben
   1 linen shroud (funeral) = 5 silver kit = 50 copper deben
   1 simple coffin = 20-40 copper deben
   1 scribe's coffin = 200 copper deben
   1 'Book of the Dead' = 100 copper deben

Animals
   1 goat = 2½ copper deben
   1 donkey = 25-40 copper deben
   1 cow = up to 140 copper deben
   1 bull = 50-120 copper deben
   1 ox = 60 copper deben

Slaves and other
   1 slave girl = 4 silver deben
   1 ordinary male slave = 3 silver deben + 1 silver kit

Table 19 (continued)

Metals (approximate values)
1 gold kit = 2 silver kit = 200 copper kit
1 kit = 9.4 g
1 deben = 91 g Copper
1 seniu = 1/12 deben (in weight) = 7.6 g silver = *c.* 8 copper deben
(728g); 3½ seniu = *c.* 30 deben

Index of Place Names

Index of Place Names